Structural Macroeconomic Change and the Size Pattern of Manufacturing Firms

Structural Macroeconomic Change and the Size Pattern of Manufacturing Firms

Fabrizio Traù
Research Department of the Confederation of Italian Industries
Rome, Italy

palgrave
macmillan

First published 2003 by
PALGRAVE MACMILLAN
Houndmills, Basingstoke, Hampshire RG21 6XS and
175 Fifth Avenue, New York, N.Y. 10010
Companies and representatives throughout the world

PALGRAVE MACMILLAN is the global academic imprint of the Palgrave Macmillan division of St. Martin's Press, LLC and of Palgrave Macmillan Ltd. Macmillan® is a registered trademark in the United States, United Kingdom and other countries. Palgrave is a registered trademark in the European Union and other countries.

ISBN 1–4039–1804–X

This book is printed on paper suitable for recycling and made from fully managed and sustained forest sources.

A catalogue record for this book is available from the British Library.

Library of Congress Cataloging-in-Publication Data
Traù, Fabrizio.
    Structural macroeconomic change and the size pattern of manufacturing firms / Fabrizio Traù.
        p. cm.
    Includes bibliographical references and index.
    ISBN 1–4039–1804–X (cloth)
        1. Business enterprises – Size. 2. Small business. 3. Macroeconomics.
    I. Title.

HD69.S5T73 2003
338.6'4—dc21   2003051178

10 9 8 7 6 5 4 3 2 1
12 11 10 09 08 07 06 05 04 03

Printed and bound in Great Britain by
Antony Rowe Ltd, Chippenham and Eastbourne

A Gastone

Contents

List of Tables

List of Figures

Acknowledgements

This book is the outcome of several years of reflection about the changes in the organization of industrial activities experienced by developed countries in the last decades of the twentieth century. Its main focus is on the economic relationship between the crisis of the "Golden Age" regime and the reversal of the trend towards increasing business concentration it contributed to foster over the first phase of post-war industrial development. From this point of view, it may be considered as an attempt to set the now commonly emphasized revival of "small-scale production" within the wider framework of "institutional" change.

The ideas set forth here have been ripening within different research contexts. The question of the effects of structural change on firm size had been first approached by myself on theoretical grounds in autumn 1997, when I was visiting the Centre for Business Research in the Department of Applied Economics at the University of Cambridge. I wish to thank Alan Hughes (CBR Director) for having made my visit possible once again, and all the CBR staff for having provided – as usual – an ideal environment in which to work. Special thanks I owe to Michael Pollitt and Frank Wilkinson for having read a first draft of a paper on the subject and provided useful comments. Financial support from the British Council has also to be gratefully acknowledged.

At the empirical level, the establishment of the data-set which constitutes the basis for the whole work has been made possible thanks to the financial and institutional support of the G. Taliercio Foundation, in the context of a research project aimed at analysing the organizational problems of small businesses in the Italian economy. This research project, which I coordinated over a one-and-a-half-year period (from spring 1998 to autumn 1999), has involved a number of scholars from various universities and research institutions; the possibility to meet them as a group several times during the course of the research work has allowed me to benefit from very stimulating discussions about the peculiar role that the small business sector has assumed in the context of the Italian industrial system, as this book will show.

Indeed, the production of an original data-set of international statistics on industrial structure – with special reference to firm size – has to be considered as an autonomous work in itself. It has required the establishment of an *ad-hoc* research group, which has carried out its work over a two-year period. All information about such activity is contained in Appendix A; but I very much wish to acknowledge here the great deal of work carried out by the members of the group: Annalisa Armanni, Raffaella Sadun and above all Anita Guelfi, who has shared with me the difficult task of approaching the problem of collecting – and harmonizing – data from the very beginning of this research. This phase of the work has also benefited from the help by Yoshiro Miwa (Tokyo University) and John Seabold (United States Bureau of Census), who have provided us with data about Japanese and US businesses, respectively. But special thanks in this connection I owe to Peter Hart, first of all for his warm encouragement, and in particular for having introduced me to the mysteries of British statistics on business units, providing clear direction in interpreting their often apparently undecypherable meaning.

In a broader perspective, the analysis of the long-run changes occurring in the industrial structure of "advanced" countries has been developed as a part of a research programme on the particular nature of Italian industrial structure – as compared to other industrialized countries – that I have been carrying out in the Research Department of the Confederation of Italian Industries (Centro Studi Confindustria) over recent years. In this connection, I should like to thank my current and former colleagues in the CSC for having helped me, through continuous discussions, to clarify (at least to some extent, I hope) my ideas about the questions at issue.

The view outlined in this work has been given the opportunity to improve its soundness (if any) in the course of a series of seminars and lectures I have given at the Universities of Parma, Pisa, Reading, Siena and Urbino; as to methodology, I have to mention the work carried out on the occasion of presenting a paper about international comparisons of business data in the course of a Conference on Business Censuses promoted by the Italian Statistical Society, held in Udine in June 1999.

Individual chapters of the book have had circulation, partially in Italian and partially in English, as working papers or articles in books and journals;[1] comments on single such works and in some cases on the whole book have also been provided by Aris Accornero, Valeriano Balloni, Mark Casson, Piero Cipollone, Donato Iacobucci and Paolo Mariti. None of these people, of course, can be considered responsible for any errors or inadequacies still present in the final draft. Specific mention, moreover, I have to make of the work by Giovanni Foresti, who has reviewed the whole book in order to verify the overall consistency of the empirical findings, and by Giuliana Timpani, for very helpful assistance in editing tables and figures.

Finally, I really wish to stress here the invaluable role played by Alessandro Arrighetti in having helped me to gradually focus the very core of the arguments analysed in this book, in the course of innumerable discussions on the matter (and related issues) we have been involved in since our first meeting in Cambridge in 1994. This is not a debt; I have simply to say that, in some cases, I hardly can identify where his ideas end, and mine start.

Introduction

He said, it was very reasonable to think ... that there must have been Giants in former Ages (...). He argued, that the very Laws of Nature absolutely required we should have been made in the Beginning, of a Size more large and robust ...

(J. Swift, *Gulliver's Travels*)

In the early 1980s a growing body of literature began to draw the attention of economic analysts and policy-makers to the "new" role played by small businesses in the context of industrial production. The developments of the literature on the matter – not always supported by reliable empirical evidence – led quickly to the establishment of a new standpoint, which viewed the phenomenon as a sharp reversal of the previous trend towards the concentration of production activities within giant enterprises, which would herald a future characterized by an increased role for small-scale production. By the end of the century a widespread belief had grown among many institutions and a growing number of scholars that the industrial system was probably to be considered as being at the outset of a new era of small, customer-oriented manufacturing activities which would quickly sweep away the remnants of the mass production system.[1]

Indeed, as this book tries to illustrate, employing a new data-set which has allowed a much wider examination of the phenomenon than hitherto (below, see chapters 3 to 5), the post-Second World War period seems to have been characterized in industrial countries by a major break in the evolutionary pattern of firms' size structure. During the 1970s, the trend towards growing concentration (with a rising average size of enterprises) inherited from the pre-war period came to a halt, and was followed by a sharp reversal. Since then, the average size of firms has begun to fall, and the employment share of smaller firms has risen. In a long-run perspective, a "V" pattern of the importance (of the weight) of smaller firms seems to be at work; in structural terms, this has represented one of the most relevant features of industrial development in the last thirty years.

Yet, showing that the alleged change in industrial structure did actually take place, as we do here, is not the end of the matter. Indeed, on "historical" grounds, it would be hard to think of such an apparent discontinuity as if it were independent of the important changes which have characterized the economic environment over the same period. And, admittedly, from this point of view economic literature has occasionally highlighted the relevance of several factors that have contributed to modify the economic conditions firms have to cope with when taking decisions. Among them are the emerging need for product differentiation brought about by rising income levels (acting against large-scale product standardization), the major technological breakthrough represented by "flexible" technologies (lowering the minimum efficient size of plants), the outbreak of job actions (fostering the decentralization of production towards smaller – i.e. "less unionized" – units), and the oil shocks of the 1970s, which have discouraged the sort of energy-intensive production methods that are usually associated with large-scale plants.[2]

Nevertheless, after having considered all these phenomena, we still have to conclude that, even viewed in merely historical terms, there is a great deal more to take into account. In particular, the above mentioned explanations for "the re-emergence of small-scale production" seem to have neglected important changes that have affected firms' behaviour at the macroeconomic level. This neglect (reflecting the natural "orientation" of macroeconomists towards short-term analysis) obscures, in particular, the role played by the exhausting of the "historical aberration" of the Golden Age. That is, by the crisis of the economic regime which for a couple of decades (the 1950s and the 1960s) represented – through a steady growth of demand and exceptionally high investment rates – the engine of an unprecedented phase of economic growth of advanced industrial countries.[3]

From the point of view of this volume, among the factors that lie behind the "fall of the Golden Age" there are at least two major phenomena which have to be stressed when firms' changing behaviour is being considered: namely, the strengthening of competition brought about by the increased importance of external demand (which in some respects may be considered as a consequence of the "success" of the

Golden Age itself), and the rising uncertainty (coupled with slower growth rates) which has followed the crisis of the Bretton Woods system and the abandoning of fixed exchange rates.[4]

As far as the first phenomenon is concerned, we can consider economic integration through international trade as being the "natural" outcome of the growth of the industrial sector in advanced countries. With regard to the second, it can be said that the most apparent difference between the Golden Age years and the more recent phase of economic development in advanced countries lies precisely in the transition from a regime in which such economies were extensively regulated both externally and internally, to a situation in which financial liberalization and globalization create "new" scope for speculation, leading in turn to a high level of volatility in macroeconomic variables.

The thesis set forth in the first chapter of this book is that these factors have resulted in a substantial change in firms' "environment", fostering a gradual tendency towards lower organizational complexity and diversification. Viewed from such a perspective this volume may be considered as an attempt to build a bridge between two important phenomena which have characterized the evolution of most industrial countries over the second half of the twentieth century, each having had their turning point around the mid-1970s: the development (and the crisis) of the macroeconomic environment set up after the Second World War; and the inversion in the pattern of development of the size structure of industrial firms we referred to above, first oriented towards the growing significance of big business, and then being characterized by a greater role for smaller companies.

But this does not exhaust the issue. In fact, in order to understand the nature of the changes at issue a further step is needed, which asks us to search in economic theory for the possible explanations for these phenomena to coincide in time: that is, to find out which *theoretical* view of firm's behaviour may help us to explain why, in the face of *those specific* macroeconomic changes, business firms have *actually* decided to give *that* kind of organizational answer to the problem of production. An attempt to answer this question is contained in chapter 2. In this connection, it is suggested that, building on the work of Richardson (1960), Malmgren (1961) and Robinson (1935), it is possible to develop a framework which can help us to explain in a single theory the changing logic of firms' behaviour in the face of the passage from the Golden Age to the "Restructuring" phase which took place around the early 1970s. In the second phase, our theoretical view suggests that in the face of a *twofold* shock, affecting the economic system in terms of *both* higher uncertainty and rising competition, the need to manage a growing amount of information *and* simultaneously to become more efficient leads the firm, given the amount of managerial resources it has at its disposal, to an overall *reduction* in its size. This takes place on one side through the shedding of non-core competencies, in order to concentrate on those activities in which the firm has the greatest comparative advantage; on the other, through vertical dis-integration, driven by the need to make the organization "less complex" by reducing the relative weight of fixed costs. The overall result is a fall in the transactions which take place within larger businesses.

As we have said, chapters 3 to 5 give empirical substance to the actual changes that have occurred in the post-war years in the size structure of manufacturing business units, viewed as the outcome of changes in the organization of production activities over the same period. In this connection our empirical analysis hinges upon the ad hoc construction of a new data-set, based on primary (national) sources, which provides information at the two-digit (Isic Rev.2) sectoral level for six industrial countries (France, Germany, Italy, Japan, the United Kingdom and the United States).

After having surveyed current literature about the changes affecting the size structure of industrial countries in the last years of the twentieth century, chapter 3 provides an overall description of the employment shifts (in both relative and absolute terms) which can be observed in two different phases of the post-war period (the "Golden Age" years from the early 1960s to the mid-1970s, and the "Restructuring" period from the mid-1970s to the early 1990s). In chapter 4, the view outlined in chapters 1 and 2 (involving an overall trend towards vertical and conglomeral dis-integration of the industrial structure) is considered in the light of more dis-aggregated data, by distinguishing between employment changes driven by variations in the average size of business units (characterized by an upward trend in the first phase and a fall in the second one) and changes due to variations in their overall numbers (showing an opposite trend).

Finally, in chapter 5 specific attention is paid to the differences which can be found in the behaviour of business firms as opposed to establishments. This emphasis reflects the belief that the above mentioned macroeconomic changes, by their very nature, should have more effect on the scale of *organizational* structures – whilst it is far less clear, in the light of those changes, which overall trend we should expect to find out in those *technical* units which can be broadly termed as plants. In this respect, the analysis developed in chapter 5 concentrates upon the empirical implications of a major issue which is first addressed on theoretical grounds in chapter 2: namely, the fact that as firms get larger, they change *in shape*, and not just in size, by becoming more and more complex entities, and seeing a decline in the share of resources devoted solely to *productive* activities. This points, in itself, to a more general issue: that is, the fact that whereas a proper understanding of the matter would require a *specific* treatment of the behaviour of the firm as an *organization*, such a kind of requirement is precisely what standard economic theory, by its very nature, does its best to ignore – insofar as admitting that things happen inside the firm, which do not simply reflect a mechanical response to market impulses given by 'a "bodyless" economic agent', would run against the general equilibrium view of competition.[5] From this point of view, the analysis developed in chapter 5 emphasizes that the nature of structural changes in the size pattern cannot be understood without taking into account the fact that they reflect changes in the *internal* organization of business units.

Indeed, as it relates to the plan of the book, it might appear a somewhat odd choice to set the description of the actual trends in size structure – that is, the very issue to be interpreted – *after* those chapters that aim to provide an overall interpretation of the mechanisms on which they depend. In a sense, this means asking the reader to take for granted, in the first two chapters, the analysis which has still to be demonstrated. From this point of view it has to be said that the sequence of the chapters in the book simply reflects the *causal* link between the two phenomena under observation: in this perspective, we discuss macroeconomic changes first, because *they* represent the strongest force pushing towards vertical dis-integration – and therefore to changing firm size structure. However, insofar as we cannot take into account such forces without explaining the logic of firm behaviour, theory must follow closely: so the three chapters devoted to the illustration of the available empirical evidence can only come *after* two chapters in which their overall determinants have been explained.

The story developed in this book has probably come to an end in recent years: by the late 1990s, increasing evidence of a new trend towards rising concentration – at least at the financial level – is often claimed to have been emerging in many countries. Moreover, the nature itself of what we traditionally call business firms seems to have lost some of its meaning, their boundaries having somewhat blurred in the face of ever looser definitions of the entities which carry out the various phases of the process leading from production to the market.

Yet, the worst that could be done in this connection would be trying to infer, from the relatively sparse empirical evidence we currently possess for these more recent years, the lines of a "new industrial pattern" for the years to come. As the spectacular failure of many recent attempts to identify in a few facts the paradigm of a "new economy" shows beyond any reasonable doubt,[6] nothing is more risky than assuming that what is happening now (if any different pattern is actually emerging) can be taken as the watershed to a new era of industrial development.

1

The Macroeconomic Context in Historical Perspective: Exogenous and Endogenous Changes in Firms' 'Competitive Environment'

1.1 Golden Age, industrial development, big business

1.1.1 Towards the end of the 1960s, J.K. Galbraith began his analysis of the working of the "New Industrial State" with the blunt remark that "the part of the economy ... of which the most conspicuous manifestation is the modern big corporation ... is the part ... we identify with the modern industrial society ... To understand the rest of the economy ... is to understand very little" (Galbraith 1967, p. 9).[1]

It can be said that at the time Galbraith's view reflected, from an empirical standpoint, the apparent absence of *economic* forces which could resist the rise of large corporations as the dominant element within the production system: regardless of whether it was actually bound to culminate in the dominance of the "technostructure" over the organization of production and trade, the *fact* that production was concentrating in ever larger and more complex corporations appeared – albeit with some reservations[2] – simply to be one of the *immanent* laws of industrial development itself. On the other hand, the growing size (and influence) of large corporations in the economies of industrial countries had already resulted, at the time, in several attempts to provide an explanation of the phenomenon on theoretical grounds; so that, from this point of view, the early 1960s coincide with the emergence of several "models" that aimed to explain the internal functioning of large firms.[3]

If the emphasis on concentration as such harks back to the analysis of Marx, the crucial reference on which the whole set of these theoretical constructions is grounded is undoubtedly that of Berle and Means (1932): the main axis on which the different contributions hinge is that of the progressive "managerialization" of large corporations, triggered off by the separation of ownership and control. But in this connection a fundamental role – somehow a preliminary one – is played by the developments of organizational theories, which since the early post-war years have been a major arena for the analysis of the decision-making system (especially discretionary behaviour) within complex bureaucracies.[4]

A common feature of the so-called "managerial" models, from our standpoint, is that they refer to business organizations as entities which – by their very size – are less and less affected by the constraints typical of a competitive market, and which have in fact a growing control over the demand for their products and the supply of inputs required to run their business. Their ability to make the competitive environment somewhat more "stable" is accompanied by the tendency to make decisions within a framework of long-term strategies – that is, on the basis of a "interconnected process of choices linked in a sequential frame spanning over a long time".[5] The inherent *dependence* of each decision upon the whole sequence of decisions taken at any one time requires the firm to operate in a context of substantial *certainty*: that is, the planning of activities must be accompanied by the phasing out of "risk components linked to external variables which were the main justification for the *entrepreneurial* power of the past".[6]

It is in these conditions that the organizational structure gradually adjusts to a "procedural" logic: to the extent that external context is characterized by a high degree of certainty with regard to the short-term behaviour of macroeconomic variables, the decision-making system may be handed over to *managers*. A given problem will be dealt with in the same way by *all* the managers who will be in charge of *that* procedure at the relevant time.

1.1.2   But neither market power nor the surfacing of a discretionary behaviour on the part of management can provide *on their own* an explanation for the establishment of the planning process of the large firm. From this point of view, the development of the corporate economy cannot be understood without accounting for the crucial role which the *macroeconomic* context played throughout the two post-war decades in ensuring optimal growth conditions for big business.

Following Glyn *et al.* (1990), it can be said that from the end of the Second World War to the end of the 1960s the economy of the industrialized countries was characterized by a phase of extraordinary growth (a veritable Golden Age) which manifested itself both in an exceptionally high level and a quite low variability over time of output growth rates. This phenomenon crucially hinged upon two factors: on the real side of the economy, the fact that during this period most developed countries were still going through an industrialization stage in terms of their growth pattern; on the financial side, the very existence of a network of institutions entrusted with the task of overseeing the trade system and capital movements, which for many years ensured a high stability of both exchange and interest rates.

With regard to the first issue, considerable attention must be paid to the strength of the unprecedented growth in the (mainly domestic) demand for consumer goods which lasted for the first two post-war decades.[7] Consumption growth did not simply help to keep aggregate demand high, it also – and perhaps chiefly – had to do with "the assurance it gave to those taking investment decisions of a *steadily* growing market", so as to foster "a general encouragement to *capacity-expanding* investment" (Glyn *et al.*, 1990 pp. 50 and 58, emphasis added). As to the financial system, it is important to remember the role played by the Bretton Woods agreements in keeping the economic relevance of speculation down to a minimum (thus contributing to the containment of costs for gathering information *outside* the enterprise[8]), and in ensuring a "reasonable predictability" of expected returns (also due to relatively low real interest rates, owing to the virtual absence of inflation risks).

In such a situation the main problem for an enterprise is to make more stable not its final *demand* – which is in itself quite stable – but rather factor *supply*, which can be adversely affected by "excessive" dependence on intermediate markets. In this context, the minimizing of risk is achieved by ensuring that access both to supply and sale channels (upstream and downstream activities) is not upset by occasional interruptions due to "market" shocks; that is, it requires the enterprise to *integrate* within one single organizational unit all the activities which its management capacity allows it to govern. As has been stressed by Chandler and Hikino (1997, pp. 29–30), in that context "potential cost advantages of plant size ... could not be fully realized unless a steady flow of materials through the plant and factory was attained"; so that "where essential supplies of raw and intermediate materials were not readily available, firms had to integrate backward into such industries and activities". Thus, growth occurs through a process of vertical integration, which responds to the need to increase the enterprise's direct control over the largest possible number of activities functionally linked to core business.[9]

Diversification of activities is, in any case, the most efficient mechanism for risk reduction in an "environmental" context characterized by a high "degree of predictability" of future events; so that in the same perspective we can look at the diffusion of the conglomerate firm, that is the entry into activities not linked to the core business – which via *external* growth fosters the trend towards growing average size of firms.[10]

The combined effects of vertical and "lateral" integration[11] bring about relevant organizational changes: as the span of control (the maximum number of people that can be directly controlled by any level of the hierarchy) is in any case limited, growth forces firms to adopt solutions which are different from the simple sequential addition of new production units, all placed within the same administrative boundaries. This is the premise for the transformation of firms into M-form organizations, which in the early 1970s become common to almost all industrialized countries – other than to those, such as the United States, where large companies had already developed.[12] In most industrial countries, but especially in the United States and in the United Kingdom, this phenomenon was accompanied by a spate of mergers and acquisitions, which since the 1960s have led to a growing number of conglomerates.[13]

1.2   The changing "competitive environment" in the early 1970s: exogenous and endogenous forces at work

1.2.1   In the early 1970s, the macroeconomic context underwent some crucial changes. These were partly exogenous (insofar as they were linked to the shocks affecting industrial economies from 1971 onwards) and partly endogenous, reflecting the very consequences (the "success") of the extraordinary period of growth spanning the 1950s and 1960s. Starting from the latter, the first thing that can be said is that the achievement of a higher degree of development implies a major change in the structure of demand. More specifically, it implies a gradual shift of the final demand towards ever less standardized and ever more diversified goods. The growing diversification reduces the economies of mass production,[14] and makes it more and more difficult to predict the dynamics of future demand.

But an even more important consequence of the "historical aberration" represented by the Golden Age, from our point of view, is the gradual but relentless international integration of business activities brought about by the very growth of industrial countries, determining an expansion of international trade faster than output growth (Figure 1.1).[15] This phenomenon – which simply mirrors the industrialization process of such countries – involves both rising shares for external supply on internal markets, and tougher competition for domestic supply on international markets, thereby determining in time a structural tightening in the level of overall market competition. From a situation where demand mainly arises in the domestic market[16] a change occurs whereby a growing share of consumption (a) depends on a growing number of producers and (b) is more and more affected by exchange rates and price fluctuations.

Increasing competition has two main effects on the pattern of development of the industrial system. On the one hand, it imposes ever more rigid constraints in terms of costs, which induce enterprises to reduce their "X-inefficiencies", thereby determining a downsizing effect due to the elimination of all the resources involved in carrying out "marginal" activities (especially as far as staff is concerned).[17] At the same time it makes it increasingly difficult for business to conduct all

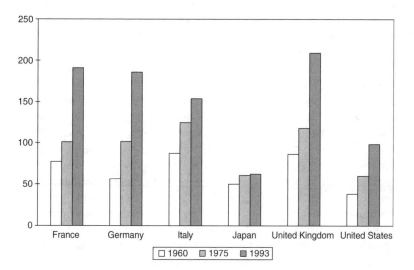

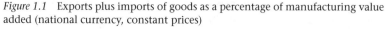

Figure 1.1 Exports plus imports of goods as a percentage of manufacturing value added (national currency, constant prices)

Source: IMF, *International Financial Statistics.*

those activities falling outside the boundaries of the *competencies* of the firm itself.[18] As has been pointed out by Carlsson (1996), in the new situation "diversification was no longer the appropriate strategy ... Increased competition made it difficult to maintain strong competitive positions in a variety of products *as the competence of management was stretched to the limit"*, for "the more diversified the firms, the less likely it is to possess the unique competence required for survival in each business unit" (pp. 80–1, emphasis added).

Downsizing therefore occurs along two lines: the first is the reduction in factor endowments per unit of output (an increase in efficiency) with no change in the "organizational complexity"; the second has to do with the reduction of such complexity, via a lower degree of *conglomerate* integration. In organizational terms, the big multidivisional firm is ready to be broken down into *autonomous* units.

1.2.2 A growing dependence on foreign demand and greater market uncertainty contributed to emphasize the impact of exogenous shocks which, in turn, began to affect the economy of industrial countries at the beginning of the 1970s. As far as the real side of the economy is concerned, the heaviest blows were dealt in 1973 and 1979 by the two oil shocks, which – besides accelerating an inflationary process that had already been started by the rigidity of real wages – pushed up relative input prices in more energy-intensive industries, generally characterized by large firms.

Yet, even more crucial problems emerged at the financial level between 1971 and 1973, when the end of the Bretton Woods system gave way to a long phase of turbulence on the exchange-rate markets, ushering in a period of considerable financial instability and increased speculation (both emphasized by the phasing out of restrictions on capital mobility in most industrial countries).[19] In macroeconomic terms this led to a considerable increase in the volatility of exchange rates and interest rates (Figure 1.2 and Table 1.1), bringing about considerable changes in firms' investment strategies: on the one hand, investment decisions are faced with an upsurge of the costs of gathering "external" information, as a growing share of resources must be allotted to the management of assets and liabilities; on the other, they are faced with the shortening of the time firms have at their disposal to take decisions.

Since the early 1980s this growing uncertainty has been compounded by the effect of the strong increase in real interest rates triggered off by policies aimed at curbing inflation (see again Table 1.1), which favoured a more general propensity to limiting investment.

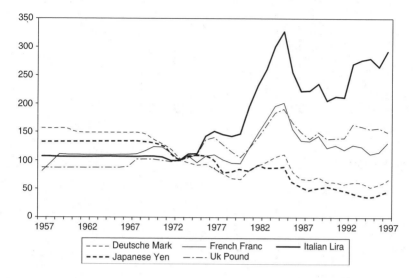

Figure 1.2 Bilateral exchange rates against the US dollar (indices 1973 = 100)
Source: IMF, *International Financial Statistics*.

Increasing costs arising from bearing higher exchange risk,[20] monitoring (more volatile) prices, facing (wider) demand fluctuations and the like mean that evaluating future returns to investments becomes more and more difficult. In a similar context, the principle applies according to which "greater uncertainty affecting the future returns to private investments, subject to sunk costs, increases the *option value of waiting*", that is to say "short-termism in the private sector is the rational private sector response to macroeconomic instability" (Buiter *et al.*, 1997, pp. 13–14, emphasis added). And since the larger the investment, the higher its sunk costs, expanding capacity will be discouraged to the extent that its scale gets greater.

Hence, the whole macroeconomic scenario tends to become hostile to long-term investment decisions – which are the very premises for large firms to *plan* their activity. Following Carlsson (1996) again, the outbreak of financial instability means – at least for those accepting such a distinction on methodological grounds – shifting from managing risk to managing uncertainty. And whereas diversifying can well help firms to guard against market risks, inasmuch as uncertainty takes the place of risk this is no longer an appropriate strategy.[21] This has a direct impact on vertical integration, pushing firms to look for a higher degree of

Table 1.1   Annual growth rates of (long-run) interest rates and consumer prices

Countries	Interest rates				Prices			
	Average		Variance		Average		Variance	
	1957–73	1973–97	1957–73	1973–97	1957–73	1973–97	1957–73	1973–97
France	6.09	9.84	1.52	6.94	5.30	6.49	10.33	19.91
Germany	7.00	7.37	1.09	2.14	3.01	3.35	2.76	3.54
Italy	6.73	12.90	1.16	11.60	3.98	10.39	7.76	37.93
Japan	7.07[a]	6.08	0.04[a]	5.39	5.30	4.06	8.53	26.20
United Kingdom	7.17	10.96	2.84	5.86	4.45	8.36	7.53	36.53
United States	5.06	8.76	1.57	4.92	2.92	5.55	3.81	10.71

[a] 1967–1973.

Source: IMF, *International Financial Statistics.*

"flexibility". In this respect, the problem can also be viewed from the perspective suggested by Contini (1984): the fact that – following Oi (1962) – firms' cost curves are generally steeper on the left side of the MES (that is, they are characterized by a strong downward rigidity in input use) makes the risk of capital underutilization very high; in a context of strong uncertainty this encourages the contracting out of those activities that are most prone to demand shocks. With adequately developed markets for intermediate goods, such a mechanism tends to divide the "original" production unit along the lines traced by the separability of cost functions.[22] Size tends to reduce along *vertical* lines.

1.2.3 At an aggregate level, the waning of the "environmental" conditions which for more than two decades had been the backbone of the Golden Age can be seen in the drastic change which as of the early 1970s became evident in the growth rate (and its stability) of most industrial countries. Figures 1.3 and 1.4 show, respectively, the (average annual) growth rate and the inter-annual variance of manufacturing GDP for each of the countries considered, in the two major development phases of the post-war period (from 1950 to 1973 and from 1974 to 1994).

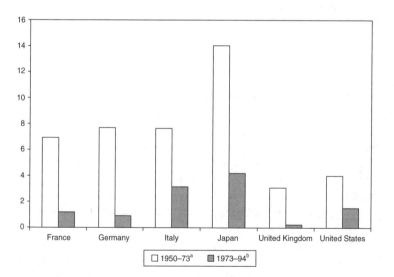

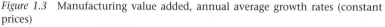

Figure 1.3 Manufacturing value added, annual average growth rates (constant prices)
[a] Italy: 1951–73; Japan 1960–73.
[b] Japan and United States: 1973–93.
Source: OECD, *National Accounts*.

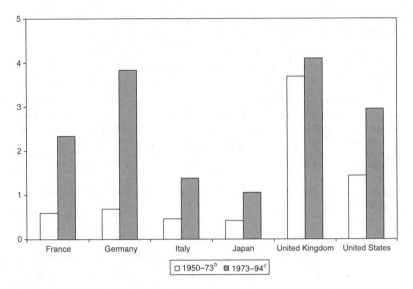

Figure 1.4   Manufacturing value added, relative standard deviation of growth rates[a] (constant prices)

[a] United Kingdom: simple s.d. × 100.
[b] Italy: 1951–1973; Japan: 1960–73.
[c] Japan and United States: 1973–93.

Source: OECD, *National Accounts*.

These figures show, without exception, that output growth suffers a notable slowdown in the years after 1973 and that this phenomenon is associated with a considerable increase in its variability.[23] Both phenomena are closely tied: higher market turbulence implies lower growth prospects, as well as more uncertain ones. But if uncertainty adversely affects growth (insofar as in the face of higher real interest rates it makes expected returns more uncertain), at the same time rising competition forces firms to focus on *optimizing*. Even if slowing down, productivity growth outpaces output growth as of the mid-1970s (Figure 1.5).

This phenomenon deserves special attention, because it suggests that – as the Golden Age was drawing to a close – a fundamental change occurred in the industrialization pattern of developed countries. The literature has discussed the slowdown of the productivity growth rate extensively on the basis of factors which can be considered more or less exogenous here (among which is the fall in the rate of output growth, coupled with rising labour rigidity). However, the most important fact in

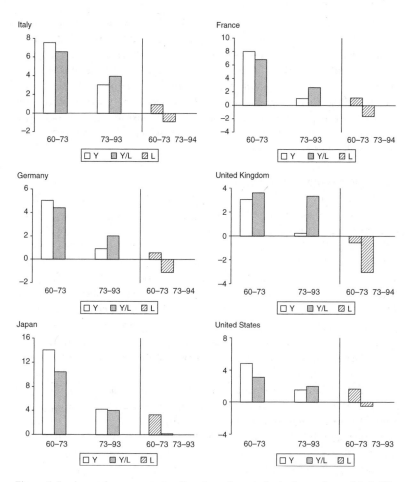

Figure 1.5   Annual average growth rates of manufacturing value added (Y), labour productivity (Y/L) and employment (L)

Source: OECD, *National Accounts*.

this context is the *reversal* of the relationship linking productivity changes to output changes: while in the period between 1950 and 1973 the former are always higher than the latter (except in the United Kingdom), in the following two decades this pattern tends to be reversed.[24]

The reversal of such a relationship involves a structural change in the growth prospects of the industrial sector. At least in terms of employment (that is, in terms of one input), the industrial base can expand only if growth is faster than technological progress. When this is no longer possible, the growth model simply changes: as Figure 1.5 shows, the need to reduce inputs per unit of production by definition translates into a sharp drop in manufacturing employment in absolute terms (with the partial exception of Japan).[25] While uncertainty discourages growth, increasing competitive pressure gradually forces out of business that part of the industrial sector which had been shielded hitherto by an exceptionally favourable market situation.

1.2.4   It has often been claimed that the shift from the Golden Age to the more recent development stage of the industrial economies has been (more or less) strongly conditioned by a further (exogenous) factor acting on the supply side. According to this view, around the mid-1970s the introduction of microelectronics into the production processes of a growing number of manufacturing activities determined a fundamental change in the long-run cost curves of firms, opening the way to a gradual reduction of the minimum efficient (plant) size. Following Steindl (1945), it could be said that this phenomenon relaxed the technological constraint due to the supposed existence of technological indivisibilities, according to which smaller-sized units are cut away from (at least some of) the most efficient production solutions. The technological advancement favoured by the introduction of the new technologies should then have narrowed – sometimes even bridged – the gap between larger and smaller firms, making the primacy of large plants over "technical" requirements no longer inevitable.[26]

In fact, empirical evidence seems to show that some (positive) relationship between the diffusion of microelectronics and the falling average size of business units can be found in the available data.[27] But the whole question deserves greater attention in analytical terms. In particular, the point here is that technology has (mostly) to do with *production*. That is, it can affect the firm's size only *indirectly* – inasmuch as it affects the size of its production units. In the perspective suggested by Steindl, this means that – at least over the historical period we are dealing with – technology basically acts on *plants*.

When it comes to the efficiency of *machinery* – as opposed to that of the *whole firm*, i.e. of the entire *organization* of business activities – optimizing becomes a purely *technical* problem, whereas in the context of the present work the very crucial issue – as size is concerned – rather lies in the way of setting (co-ordinating) each "unit"[28] within the boundaries of the same *enterprise*.[29] As has been argued so far, what is relevant from our point of view – quite apart from how much the size of plants may be affected by technical progress – is the extent to which firms are able (find it convenient) to "take their different functions together" (which may obviously be extended to include activities which are not directly related to manufacturing, as being carried out within other units). In this respect, while it may well have favoured the setting up of *new* small (single-plant) firms, technology has probably played a negligible role in the *emerging* search for vertical dis-integration, around the mid-1970s, by *existing large firms* – when microelectronics was still mainly incorporated in (single) *machines*. At *that* stage, the key issue was to be found – as we saw in previous sections – in the need for firms to reduce the costs for *coordinating* activities.

Be that as it may, as far as we know (see chapters 3 to 5 in this book), the structural change – in terms of downsizing – observed at *plant* level shows a rather different pattern from that seen with respect to *enterprises* – in most cases it starts *earlier* in time. This question will be further analysed below; nevertheless we can see here that no relevant structural changes at the plant level were brought about by technical change. If anything, in early industrialized countries economic forces had *already* begun to push towards the lower average size of *technical* units, some time *before* technology experienced such a sharp break.[30]

1.2.5   In this connection it must be stressed anyway that in a broader perspective – whether related to technology or not – the dominance of big business, which achieved dominance of the industrialized world throughout the first stage of post-war growth, actually *never* did apply across the board. Indeed, in many types of production the tendency towards higher concentration actually played a quite marginal role at *all* stages of industrial development.

As has been set out by Chandler, this phenomenon had already emerged during the spate of mergers which swept through the US economy at the turn of the century, when it became clear that

the new integrated mergers failed to play a dominant role in those industries where the process of manufacturing was labour-intensive, where the application of additional energy did not speed up the process, where selling required little in the way of special marketing services, *and where scheduling of production and distribution was less critical*. One or more of these characteristics occurred in the following industries: textiles, leather, lumber, clothing, hats, shoes, saddlery, furniture, carriage-making, and other wood-processing industries; cigars and many foods; simple metal fabricated products and machinery which did not require special installation, service, or credit; specialized machine tools and instruments; and printing and publishing. In these industries, *the adding, combining, and integrating of many units failed to provide any special competitive advantage* in terms of lower costs or greater customer satisfaction. In these businesses, single-unit enterprises ... continued to compete sucessfully against large integrated corporations (1978, p. 111, emphasis added).

The list made by Chandler is actually impressive: almost without exception – if anything with some addition – it corresponds to the whole set of modern industries characterized by a strong presence of small business units. This means that some sort of sectoral bias is at work in the present context, accounting for the fact that in some industries (whose economic importance has been declining in industrial countries) the large "multidivisional" enterprise actually *never* managed to achieve dominance.[31] But an even clearer evaluation of the reasons for the "incomplete dominance" of large vertically integrated businesses in manufacturing activities can be found in an extremely farsighted contribution by Meade, who, in a review of Galbraith's book on the Industrial State, observed as early as the late 1960s that

In the modern complex economy there are two forces at work. One is that which Professor Galbraith rightly emphasizes, namely the increased need for careful forward planning in a system which involves the commitment of large resources to inflexible uses over long periods of time. But there is a second and equally important trend, which he entirely neglects: namely, the increased need ... for a price mechanism, ... [which] arises because in the modern industrial system input–output relationships have become so complex and the differentiation between products (many of which are the technically sophisticated inputs of other production processes) has become so manifold that simple quantitative planning without a price or market mechanism becomes increasingly clumsy and inefficient (p. 391).

This means that, *even in the course of the Golden Age*, however large "that part of the economy which is represented by the large modern industrial corporation ... the other part of the modern economic system [was] indeed very large" (p. 378).

These claims – which might have appeared even extravagant in the historical phase when they were made – anticipated many of the changes which actually began to take place in the following years.

1.3 Industrial development after the Golden Age: vertical dis-integration and the 're-emergence' of self-employment

1.3.1 As of the late 1970s market conditions had become markedly different from those that had favoured the development of the corporate firm as the typical form taken by the organization of the industrial system. The macroeconomic context as a whole was no longer the "ideal" environment in which big business could thrive.

Following Harrigan (1983), it can be said that, as a general rule, "unless strategic requirements make full integration a necessity, firms should transfer some of the risk of vertical integration to outside parties" (p. 15). This arises simply from the premise that "full integration is a two-edged sword", for "costs that would be variable under a purchasing contract are converted to fixed costs". In particular, "full integration works best when price competition is not fierce enough for diseconomies to matter ... [and] if the environment is a stable one" (p. 17). This in turn reflects the fact that "stable environments have: low product differentiation, [and] infrequent product improvements ... Accordingly, in such environments competitive signals are clear and easily understood." On the contrary, "a volatile environment would ... be characterized by high product differentiation [and] frequent process innovations ... Such an industry would be characterized by erratic or cyclical demand" (p. 32). Hence, "less internal integration is appropriate under conditions of high uncertainty, volatility, and frequent product modification. More internal integration is appropriate when industry conditions are less volatile and uncertain" (p. 33). On the whole, we can say that "each firm that integrates tries to control its need for certainty, but if competitive conditions and demand variability become *too* unfavourable for it to endure, the firm will face increasing pressure to dis-integrate, or to retreat to lesser forms of integration" (p. 48, original emphasis).

This way of approaching the scope for vertical integration helps us set within a coherent framework the overall picture of structural change we have tried to outline above.[32] As a matter of fact, on empirical grounds it can be said that the first effect of structural change itself can be seen in a general fall in the degree of vertical integration of the industrial system, as can be measured by the ratio of value added to production.

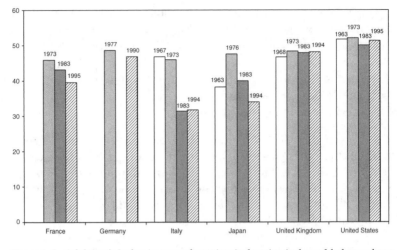

Figure 1.6   Adelman's Index in manufacturing industries (value added as a share of gross output, average of sectoral values)[a] (national currency, constant prices)
[a] See Appendix C.
Source: ONU, *Yearbook of Industrial Statistics*.

Figure 1.6 shows the long-term trend of Adelman's index[33] in manufacturing for the six countries so far considered, starting from the first year by which international statistics make it possible to venture some calculations.[34] The picture is rather clear: the degree of vertical integration tends generally to fall in the years between the mid-1970s and the early 1980s: the extent of this process varies from country to country (it reaches its maximum level in Italy and is negligible in the United Kingdom) and there seems to be an abatement (or even a reversal of the trend) in the following years. As to our discussion so far, it can be said that this evidence is compatible with the idea that the re-emergence of small-scale production was occasioned by the increase in market relations among enterprises (with "hierarchy" being gradually superseded by the market). This phenomenon seems to be coming to an end around the early 1980s: in structural terms, this could point to the fact that at this time the de-verticalization process had reached its "physiological" minimum (because the breaking down of production process could not continue forever). It should be noted, however, that as it relates to Germany the dates on which calculations can be made do not make it possible to draw precise conclusions about the matter, and that anyway the two Anglo-Saxon countries seem to be only marginally affected by the phenomenon.[35]

In this connection it can be assumed (but the question would deserve specific analysis) that in the last two countries downsizing was mainly influenced by "horizontal" de-concentration, as they were characterized by a particularly strong development of large-scale conglomerates. This hypothesis is borne out – especially as far as the US economy is concerned – by the evidence on the recent trends shown by mergers and acquisitions, which have been a quite important tool in the restructuring process of the industrial system. In fact, according to Bhagat *et al.* (1990, p. 2), towards the mid-1980s "hostile takeover activity results in allocation of assets to firms in the same industries as those assets [so that] ... by and large, hostile takeovers represent the deconglomeration of American business and a return to corporate specialization".[36] As to the fact that this phenomenon occurs in a context of *general* downsizing (at least in terms of the labour input), it can be noted that as a matter of fact "in the cases where the initial acquirer did not want the majority of the assets of the target company but only some divisions, we see a combination of a strategic acquisition *and a bustup*. ... Thus many apparent bustups turn out to be strategic in nature as well" (p. 44, emphasis added). The role that such policies might have played in favouring higher efficiency levels, on the basis of the previous remarks (see section 1.2) can also be inferred from the analysis provided by Montgomery (1994) with reference to the American economy, according to whom "on average, firms with higher levels of diversification are less profitable than firms with lower levels of diversification" and in any case "firms that diversify around specific resources are more profitable than firms that diversify more broadly" (p. 172).

1.3.2 Falling vertical integration means that manufacturing activity is divided up among a larger *number* of producers. For the market to supersede hierarchy it is necessary to start creating *new* production units – this means that a share of the economy previously controlled by managers must go back to being controlled by *entrepreneurs*. The basic lack of data which would allow an acceptable international comparison of the rate at which new firms are being created (even more difficult to find for the earliest years to be considered) makes it impossible to directly examine the phenomenon; it is, however, possible to find some indication as to the long-term trend of the share of self-employed workers with respect to total employment. In this connection, Figure 1.7 shows, from the 1960s, the trend of the ratio of self-employed workers to the total workforce in the countries considered.[37]

First of all, the figure shows the tendency of the ratio to converge across countries during the period considered. Faced with a range of

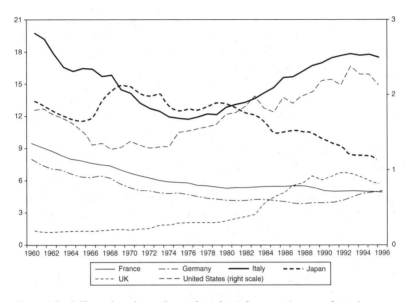

Figure 1.7   Self-employed as a share of total employment in manufacturing
Source: OECD, *Labour Force Statistics.*

over 20 percentage points in 1960, by the mid-1990s the gap between
the different countries appears to have more than halved. This phenomenon is due, on the one hand, to the drop in the index in laggard
industrialized countries (Japan and Italy, where it starts to increase again
at the end of the 1970s) and on the other hand to its increase – more or
less from the mid-1970s – in countries which developed their industrial
system first (United Kingdom and United States).

When set against the basically stationary trend of the two 'intermediate'
countries (that is, Germany and France, after a period of decrease which
lasted until the mid-1970s), this evidence suggests that in the course of
industrial development the share of self-employment tends first to show
a downward trend and then to increase.[38] In the first stage the effect of
"pre-modern" handicraft units going out of business prevails (as well as
the fact that their self-employed workers become the employees of larger
firms). During the second stage the very forces reducing the profitability
of large-scale production (thereby causing downsizing) are once again
inducing many employees to turn to self-employment.[39]

Coming back to an organization of the production process which
enhances the role of the entrepreneur – through the shrinking of that

part of the economy (the big business sector) where *management* influence is greater – tilts the balance of the decision-making system in favour of production units less prone to *internal* conflicts. A growing *share* of decision-making units with a low degree of organizational complexity in turn brings about an overall reduction of the "extra" costs required to manage internal conflicts (and therefore of the *time* required to take decisions); that is, those costs which – other things being equal – tend to increase the costs of "hierarchies" as opposed to those of the market (see below, section 2.2).[40]

The analysis outlined in the previous pages suggests that the prerequisite for this to happen must be sought in the fact that "hierarchy" costs are lower than "planning economies" only as long as market uncertainty and competition are so limited as to reduce the risks of capital underutilization to a minimum. According to this view – albeit to a different extent in different countries – downsizing and the employment shift towards smaller firms are two facets of one and the same phenomenon.

1.4 In summary

The last quarter of the twentieth century saw the re-emergence of a way of organizing production and trade based on a high degree of division of labour *among* firms (rather than *within* them). This phenomenon represents a major reversal with respect to what only thirty years ago appeared to be the only possible form of development of the industrial system: namely, the primacy of large business organizations characterized by a high degree of both vertical and conglomerate integration. Along with Simon (1991)[41] we can say that the *market* economy claimed back its role from the "*organizational*" economy; that is to say – in the words of Meade (1968) – that the organization of production activities readjusted the balance which set "careful forward planning" against the "price mechanism" in favour of the latter.

The break with the past introduced by this change was caused by major events that, from the end of the 1960s, affected the economies of industrialized countries on both endogenous and exogenous grounds. Current literature lists among the endogenous factors the demand shock resulting from the very mechanism of industrial development (which in itself caused consumption to move away from the typical goods of mass production), and the growing rigidity of labour, due to the achievement of full employment on the one hand (which raised the frequency and the intensity of labour conflicts within firms) and to the ever-growing standardization of work functions on the other (which lowered labour flexibility). Among exogenous shocks some attention should be paid to the consequences of the introduction into the production process of new technologies, which contributed to a reduction in the minimum efficient size of plants. But a relevant role has also to be ascribed to the asymmetric nature of oil shocks, which supposedly disadvantaged more energy-intensive industries (mostly characterized by a high average size of firms).

The role played by these factors in determining an overall decline in the relative efficiency of large-scale production was undoubtedly important. Yet, the full scope of the structural change cannot be understood without also taking into account the extraordinary "environmental" change brought about – at the macroeconomic level – by two decisive forces, both basically endogenous in nature: first, the gradual but relentless increase in competitive pressures induced by the process of international economic integration; second, the increased uncertainty on financial markets following the crisis of the Bretton Woods system.

In this chapter it has been argued that the industrial development pattern which reached its maturity at the end of the 1960s hinged upon two crucial pivots, which characterized what has been defined as the Golden Age of industrial economies: on the one hand, the strong growth of domestic consumption of industrial goods (most of these economies were still going through an industrialization stage, whereas their international integration was still relatively limited); on the other, the stability of exchange rates, interest rates and growth expectations ensured by an international financial system in which the scope for speculation was kept to a minimum. The stability (and strength) of the growth process favoured by such macroeconomic conditions induced firms to look for a higher degree of stability of supply rather than fretting about the demand side – and at the same time ensured a "reasonable predictability" of expected returns on large-scale investment plans. This translated into an overall tendency towards increasing concentration (both along vertical and horizontal lines), entailing a constant increase in the average size of firms and in their output and employment shares.

Towards the end of the 1960s that world was falling apart under the weight of its own strength. On the one side, the increase in competitive pressures brought about by the rising business integration of industrialized economies (which in its turn is a function of their degree of development) forced firms to concentrate on their core competencies – in most cases making use of a lower amount of resources (especially labour). On the other, the crisis of the international financial system shifted on to the private sector the burden of the exchange-rate risk and – due to increased inflation – emphasized the problem of interest-rate fluctuations, thereby increasing the degree of market turbulence in structural terms and paving the way to speculation, which eventually ushered in a phase of veritable uncertainty.

This had devastating effects on investment activity (which are often inexplicably underestimated): as the predictability of expected returns fell, the risks inherent in larger investment projects soared. Fixed costs (increased by the greater rigidity of labour) rose substantially and the fear of capacity underutilization replaced the Golden Age fears of supply shortages. While the competition shock acts to reduce the degree of conglomerate integration of firms, the "turbulence" shock contributes to narrow vertical integration (provided cost functions are separable). At the organizational level, the change in the size pattern corresponds to the transition from a 'managerial' economy (in which the low costs of monitoring markets are compatible with the "codified" system of response typical of the hierarchical organization of business) to a type of economy in which the entrepreneur (who offers an "immediate response" in the face of uncertain events) is once again set at the very centre of the decision-making system. The market claims back its role.[42]

It may be of some interest, in this context, to recall that, in conceptual terms, the whole question raised above had been paid an explicit attention by a thinker who, as early as the first years of nineteenth century, had realized quite a few things about the functioning of the competition mechanism. Indeed, we can find in the writings of Adam Smith (even in the context of a specific reference to international trade) a clear embryonic theory of the way in which a less "static" economic order endangers the business activities of big complex organizations led by managers:

> to buy in one market, in order to sell with profit in another, when there are many competitors in both; to watch over, not only by occasional variations in the demand, but the much greater and much frequent variation in the competition, or in the supply which that demand is likely to get from other people and to suit with dexterity and judgement both the quantity and the quality of each assortment of goods to all these circumstances, is a species of warfare of which the operations are continually changing, and which can scarce ever be conducted successfully without such an unremitting exertion of vigilance and attention as cannot long be expected from the directors of a joint stock company.

And then further down the same text:

> The only trades which it seems possible for a joint stock company to
> carry out successfully, without an exclusive privilege, are those, of
> which all the operations are capable of being reduced to what is
> called *a routine, or to such a uniformity of method as admits or little or no*
> *variation* (quotation taken from the 1963 Irwin edition, pp. 265–6,
> emphasis added).

The emphasis placed here on the "unremitting exertion of vigilance"
required by the need for monitoring ever-changing quantities and prices
coincides unmistakably with the scepticism about its very compatibility
with the organizational mode of large enterprises. The stylized facts
recalled above show how the changes that swept through the economic
system between the late 1960s and the early 1970s have dramatically
increased the "vigilance requirements" per unit of output throughout
the industrialized world.

2
A Theoretical Framework

2.1 A premise

Before approaching the analysis of the structural change of firms' size pattern in an empirical perspective, we still need to give the whole concern a firmer theoretical grounding. So far, we have simply analysed the *fact* that – in the face of the *observed* changes in "institutional" (macroeconomic) conditions – firms have been, *ceteris paribus*, induced to search for changes in the organization of productive activities, *sub specie* of a reduction – in relative terms – of internal transactions, and an expansion of market exchanges.

Yet, it has to be emphasized that this does not mean that, by their very nature, the changes occurred have brought about *as such* an overall tendency towards a lower concentration of economic resources (employment) in larger units. In fact, from a theoretical standpoint this appears far from obvious, for – as will be shown in this chapter – there is more than one theoretical view of firms' behaviour according to which this should *not* have been the case. Therefore, whilst the question of to what extent a shift in the size distribution of businesses did *actually* occur will be developed in following chapters, here we will offer some more reflections about the theoretical premises that lie behind the observed changes.

From this point of view the question to be considered can be phrased as follows: from which *theoretical* standpoint do we say that *such* trends in "underlying" economic forces (at both the micro- and macroeconomic levels) should have pushed firms to behave in the way that they have actually behaved? In other words, *which "model" of the internal functioning of firms (which idea about their internal organization) do we have in mind when discussing such a change?* Or, even more directly, are we able to find *any* theoretical explanation (*given* "historical" circumstances) for "the rise and fall of the size of firms"?

2.2 The "managerial" vision

2.2.1 As has been outlined in chapter 1, continuing corporate growth, perceived as a "natural" outcome of the industrial development process itself, led in the third quarter of the twentieth century to the emergence of a large body of theoretical literature about large-scale (managerial) firms' behaviour. Since the early 1950s, reflections upon the (growing) organizational complexity of the firm have been at the root of important theoretical contributions which have highlighted the basic weakness of the traditional theory of the firm in coping with the decision processes of economic agents in the real world.[1] By the end of that decade, and more and more frequently in the 1960s, the overwhelming evidence that the large corporation was gathering importance within the industrial system in all industrial countries led to several attempts to develop a theoretical interpretation of its functioning.[2]

Following Cyert and March (1963), large corporations' behaviour may be defined as the outcome of the action of a *coalition* of individuals, each representing "different preference orderings" (that is, individual objectives). This means that the existence of internal conflict is the "natural" state in which a complex organization works (which means that the burden of dispute settling is such as to increase unit costs in comparison to simpler organizations, which by their very nature are hardly affected at all by "internal" conflicts).[3] The literature published after Berle and Means' (1932) seminal contribution highlights that in addition to these features – which in any case are a function of the organizational scale – industrial development is associated with the development of joint stock companies as the typical form of ownership. This in turn leads to the consolidation of management as an *independent* body of administration (control). As the utility function of the new (non-owner) managers is sensitive to other parameters – which, in turn, are to a greater or lesser extent a function of size – rather than to profits, most theoretical models even point to a substantial change in the very objective of the "managerial" enterprise: to the extent that the manager's viewpoint overrides the owners', a growth in size becomes one of the ends of the *enterprise*.

From the point of view of our analysis, then, the more relevant feature of the "managerial" view consists in its assumption that within the firm agents act economically, but *following quite different rules with respect to the market*. As compared to more recent treatments of the problems involved by intra-firm conflicts among (different types of) agents, this assumption presents important differences. Indeed, not only does it appear at variance with the developments of "property rights" theories (according to which the firm is simply a "nexus of contracts"),[4] but it also departs distinctly from the basic Coasian view (below, section 2.3): in fact, even if sharing important common features with that view (that is, acknowledging the existence of an "authority principle" inside the firm[5]), it goes far beyond this in its implications. The point here is that the very nature of the firm as an organization – its being constituted by different "groups" characterized by different motivations as to what kind of goals the firm has to pursue – creates the conditions whereby new functions may be integrated *even in the absence of any attempt to reduce (minimize) costs.*[6] That is, firms, according to the managerial view, may choose to expand even if transaction costs are *not* higher than the costs of carrying out the same activity within the firm: they may grow larger just because growth is by definition the long-run driving force of complex organizations as such.

2.2.2   An implicit issue in this context should be that firms have some market power (even if they do not minimize costs, they are not inexorably driven to failure by the sheer strength of the market selection mechanism). So, at any one size level, they may be larger than would be required by market rules. In a "Carnegie Mellon" view,[7] it can be said that activities carried out within (large-scale) firms are affected, by their very nature, by some degree of "organizational slack". In the words of Williamson (1964) "managerial discretion models ... are intended to apply ... where competitive conditions are not typically severe" (p. 39).

As we know, from this point of view the Golden Age regime has for many years provided the "ideal" environment within which managerial capitalism could thrive: long-run stability in prices, in exchange rates, in the growth of (internal) demand and so on may be considered to be the "natural" driving forces under which managerial (growth-maximizing) behaviour can be implemented. And as far as the institutional side is concerned, strong market regulation largely contributed to keep the limits set by "market control" on corporate behaviour as loose as possible.

But in this connection an important change is represented by the rise of competition. With its need to drive down prices, it emphasizes the need to reduce *costs*. And whatever the goals of the firm may be, when profit margins are squeezed below some "sustainable" level then *all* firms do minimize costs. As Reder put it (1947, p. 453): "in a fiercely competitive situation [the firm] ... may be unable to stand any inefficiency whatever. It is when profits turn into losses that management discovers how much inefficiency it has been tolerating and strives to eliminate it."

Hence, we are to expect that, to the extent that competition becomes tougher, "excessive" size will tend to disappear. That is, firms will first of all reduce X-inefficiencies due to low competitive pressures, and then "strive to eliminate" all the functions which involve a higher level of costs than could be attained by simply applying to the market. And indeed, we know that as far as competition has risen, it has been paralleled by a constant tendency towards a *fall* in the average size of large firms.

We can then say that "managerial" behaviour is no longer consistent with the "new" competitive environment. But neither is it very consistent with an "uncertain" environment. Discretion as such requires the possibility to make choices between alternatives, which in turn calls for adequate information; and were information inadequate (either through being limited or as a result of there being insufficient time available to take decisions) managers might be bounded to make suboptimal choices with respect to *their own* utility function. In fact, their decision process may be thwarted by the impossibility of getting a reasonable evaluation of the economic implications of long-run growth (that is, their own goal); and insofar as growth raises sunk costs (which means higher rigidity), it would be discarded in favour of more "shortsighted" objectives.

Therefore, whereas managerial theories represent a very effective theoretical framework for understanding why a long era of growing sizes of firms did actually take place, they cannot interpret what happened later (simply, in the new context managerial discretion can only apply within narrower boundaries). Therefore, we require some other theoretical view which could help us explain how firms began to behave after the Golden Age regime came to an end.

2.3 Transaction costs and beyond

2.3.1 As a general rule, we can say that according to transaction cost (TC) theories firms (organizations) take the place of the market when at the margin "market" costs are higher than the costs of keeping an activity "inside" the firm. Internal organization is the answer to relative market inefficiency, which arises as a result of the existence of bounded rationality, asset specificity, and the opportunistic behaviour of agents.[8] Yet, the fall in the average size of firms which the last quarter of the twentieth century has witnessed has in fact reflected a constant tendency towards *lower* organizational complexity, *sub specie* of a gradual *increase* in market exchanges as compared to intra-firm transactions. For TC theories to work in this connection, then, we should find that the gains from "using the market" had indeed risen considerably, over the same period (at least in relative terms), throughout the industrialized world. Or, alternatively, the organizational capability of (efficiently) governing internal transactions must have fallen. In the face of rising competition and market uncertainty, how could a (relatively) higher efficiency of the "market option" have been achieved?

As far as the first issue is concerned, it would appear almost tautological to say that – inasmuch as the degree of market regulation in most countries has been gradually eroded in the same years as vertical disintegration has taken place – the widening of market transactions is only one consequence of stronger competition. As prices have been generally pushed lower by market pressures, firms in the final stages of the production chain may well have found an incentive – other things being equal – in applying to the market for purchasing intermediate inputs, thereupon externalizing those activities which were more costly.

Nonetheless, things *cannot* have remained equal, simply because – as has already been stressed – stronger competition pushes for lower *internal* inefficiencies within *all* firms (that is, it tends to reduce the costs of carrying out the activities "inside the skin" of integrated firms as well). On the whole, whilst it says nothing about what happens to the costs of transacting through the market, an increase in competition says anyway very little about what happens to efficiency *within* organizations.[9]

On the other hand, as it relates to uncertainty, the TC view seems to have little more to say that were the environment characterized by growing "turbulence", then the costs of keeping under control prices and demand fluctuations (and possibly to face faster technological change) should *rise*, thus creating a further incentive to bring activities within the firm.

The (implicit) predictions of the "standard" TC view, therefore, seem on the whole not to tally with the *actual* direction of structural change. However, in order to discuss what may have happened to the changing boundaries between market and hierarchy, we still have to consider the role played by some other factors that seem to be rather neglected in the TC view.

2.3.2   From this point of view, we can, first, simply try to extend the basic Coase–Williamson paradigm, by taking into account some more ways in which uncertainty may affect firms' behaviour. To start with, we can draw attention on the framework suggested by Carlton (1979), according to whom 'vertical integration can be regarded as a means of transferring risk from one sector of the economy to another. Firms have an incentive to integrate to ensure a supply of input to satisfy their "high probability" demand' (p. 190).

This means that insofar as "upstream" producers within an industry must set the price of their output (that is, the input for "downstream" producers) over the level corresponding to marginal cost – as they bear the risk of having unsold stocks in a context of fluctuating demand – "downstream" producers may be induced – in order to pay for their inputs a lower price, i.e. at cost – to integrate. On the other hand, as *they* would in this case bear the risk of having unused input stocks, they may nonetheless choose to settle for a *partial* integration, corresponding to the production of inputs which they are "certain" to need – and then enter the market as far as it is required by rising demand.

This framework helps to highlight how vertical integration within an industry may be affected by variations in the "degree of predictability" of final demand. *Ceteris paribus*, in the outlined perspective "downstream" firms would set their boundaries according to the range of demand fluctuations. Size would be a function of the need for "flexibility".

Outside the sphere of TC analysis, it is possible to find similar insights about the effects of demand uncertainty upon the division of labour among firms – generally coupled with some analysis of costs rigidities – in the contributions by Mills and Schumann (1985), Carlsson (1989), Das *et al.* (1993), and, on more explicit "Stiglerian" premises, by Contini (1984). But perhaps the whole question can best be appreciated through the words of Austin Robinson, who argued (1935, pp. 85–6) that

> where an industry is subject to considerable changes of demand, due either to permanent changes of taste on the part of consumers, or to changes of the methods of production caused by improvements in the thing produced, or in the technique of producing it, that firms will be strongest which can best face the problems of reorganisation and adaptation. The more elaborate a firm is, the more highly specialised in equipment, the better adapted in lay-out to the existing rhythm of production, the more expensive and difficult will be its

re-equipment, the more complicated the task of moving and adjusting to their new functions heavy and capricious pieces of machinery.

On the other hand, "the smaller firm may be never so well adapted, but will be never so ill adapted, and will enjoy, therefore, a certain advantage where changes of product are frequently necessary, and reorganisation is expensive", so that (p. 102, emphasis added): "Our argument so far [leads] us to the conclusion that the existence of risks and fluctuations leads in general to smaller units, and in particular to smaller technical units, *than would be economical were production carried out continuously and evenly.*"

2.3.3 Considering the "flexibility" issue, it might be argued that a successful way of coping with an uncertain environment may also be achieved through a quite different way of looking at market relationships among firms; in particular, by acknowledging the central role which can be played in the face of pervasive uncertainty by firms' *cooperation*. In fact, insofar as uncertainty arises "from the problems of matching production processes to shifts in demand in intermediate and final product markets, and increases considerably to the extent that products are either customised or new, ... the avoidance of producing unsaleable stock or allowing demand to go unsatisfied requires *responsive* linkages within the chain" (Deakin and Wilkinson, 1996, p. 97, emphasis added). This means that a productive system may find a way of meeting uncertain market conditions neither through competition nor through vertical integration: in such perspective, "the notions of *cooperation* and *networks* can then be added as a third and, until recently, comparatively neglected set of alternatives" (p. 99, original emphasis).[10]

The outcome of "cooperative" behaviour – which can be further buttressed by the role institutions can play in fostering trust among economic agents – will be an organizational form which is both "flexible" and "efficient": vertical integration, as well as coordination through the market, may be replaced by an *integrated* system of *independent* firms. In this sense, its strengthening may "naturally" push towards a lower average size of firms.

Both of the "solutions" to market uncertainty outlined here are grounded on the possibility for firms to rely upon a sound "system" of market relationships with other firms. This highlights a specific point – that monitoring the market does not exhaust the activities that firms have to carry out when setting up market relations: spot transactions represent only a small fraction of overall market exchanges which firms are involved in, even for running their *current* activity. As a market relation system develops, vertical *dis*-integration may turn out to be wholly compatible with an increasingly "turbulent" environment.

On the whole, all of the arguments considered in this section refer to the role of the firm as a *production* unit.[11] But there are a number of *further* issues to be tackled when considering the firm as an *organization*.

2.3.4 As has been stressed by Simon (1991), "New Institutional" (NI) theories (broadly including TC analysis, principal–agent models and the property rights approach) retain "the centrality of market and exchanges" (p. 26). In the NI world, the firm is still viewed as a surrogate for market imperfections – at their very root, NI theories are aimed at explaining what happens when economic agents try to offset some failure in the "natural" way of making transactions throughout the economic system.

But is it possible to retain such a view of economic behaviour in a world which appears to be far more a sum of *organizations* (where "the larger part of a modern economy's business is done") than a sum of market relationships? In Simon's view, it is not;[12] and understanding "what makes organizations work as … they do" means first of all exploring what motivates people living within them. In this respect, attention must be paid to several factors which NI theories do not generally take into account. From the point of view of this work, in particular, it may be of some interest to consider the relationship between "authority" and "loyalty".

According to Simon (1945 and 1991), the authority principle (which also plays a central role in Coase's analysis) is the channel through which the basic incompleteness of the employment contract is implemented. A key issue in this framework is that for the employer one way to reduce uncertainty is to delay employees' commitments to the time when the required action will be called for; that is, "the orders will not be issued until some time after the contract is negotiated" (Simon, 1991, p. 31).[13] However, in this connection it happens that – more than specifying concrete actions – commands often do not get far beyond a broad definition of the guidelines for future action, so that "for the organization to work well, it is not enough for employees to accept commands literally" (p. 32). This means that the functioning of (complex) organizations hinges upon the fact that the acceptance of the authority principle for the employees extends up to the point that they will take initiatives *on their own* in order to achieve the organization's objectives.

In other words, employees contribute to the achievement of firms' goals much more than "the minimum which could be extracted from them".

Yet, it is not even the level of rewards which can determine employees' effort, because of the basic difficulties in attributing the success of the firm to individuals.[14] Much more than this, it is "loyalty" (in terms of identification with organizational goals) which motivates people to assume responsibility – and not to simply "follow the rules" – for achieving results.[15]

A similar point is made by Casson (1991), according to whom "the firm needs an ethic of achievement to motivate technologically independent workers, and a sense of team spirit, based on shared objectives, to prevent a weak link developing in a team" (p. 233). Casson's analysis is also relevant to the above perspective because it assumes that there is a structural difference in the way in which motivation is influenced in "small" and "big" firms: while in small firms involvement occurs through direct contact with the managers of the organization, so that "each follower is allowed to respond in his own idiosyncratic way", in big firms an organization is needed in which "followers ... are required to answer in a standardized format" (p. 177). In this context, standardization is necessary due to the fact that "in a larger group the role of personal example is diminished", but it implies a trivialization of "messages" and therefore their increasing ineffectiveness.

In a broader perspective, tackling the issue of the impact which "team spirit" exerts on the overall performance of business firms almost naturally leads us to mention the approach developed by E. Mayo and his "Human Relations" School (see Mayo, 1933), according to which economic incentives do not play an exclusive role in determining workers' performance: human behaviour inside organizations depends significantly upon the nature of the relationships linking any single worker to the "group" to which he belongs.

Even if it appears to be quite difficult to evaluate the role that any "structural" changes in motivation may have played in affecting the ability of organizations to carry out their activities, it can nevertheless be acknowledged that the last quarter of the twentieth century witnessed a sharp change in the perception of authority and loyalty on the part of people working within organizations.[16] As the Golden Age of industrial economies was drawing to a close – and quite simultaneously with the outbreak of market uncertainty we accounted for in chapter 1 above, which would have required in itself a highly "flexible" behaviour aimed at facing fast-changing events – firms were to suffer the impact of a clear drop in employees' propensity to tackle management problems outside the usual way of a "routine" perspective. Vertical dis-integration may then have been influenced by the weakening of one of the forces which work to keep the organization together.[17]

2.4   Organizational complexity, information, "internal" resources

2.4.1   A consideration of the firm from an organizational point of view involves a particular emphasis, in the light of the above mentioned "environmental" changes, on the role played by information.

According to this perspective, we can start from the point that for business organizations a more uncertain environment has meant an increased need for information. As we have seen (chapter 1), due to the rising short-term volatility of exchange and interest rates and demand, firms have had to devote an increasing share of internal resources to monitoring markets. In this sense, the cost of using the market (in terms of gathering adequate information) for the individual firm should have *increased* during this period.

Following Malmgren (1961), we can observe in this respect that in the presence of uncertainty about the future state of events, putting any activity under the control of the organization in order to "reduce the fluctuations in required information" – as would be required by the Coase–Williamson paradigm – is subject to an important restriction: this can be expressed, in Malmgren's own words, by saying that "internal knowledge is definitive in forming its expectations only if the firm is in no way dependent upon expectations and plans *elsewhere in the market*" (p. 408, emphasis added). From this point of view, Malmgren pays a great deal of attention to the framework provided by G.B. Richardson (1960), and in particular to the emphasis he places on the relevance which the control of information can assume in managing what happens *outside* the boundaries of firms. According to this view, a crucial issue is represented by the fact that firms' control only applies to information about variables which are *independent of the market*.[18] Hence, as firms also have to cope with "secondary information" (which relates to what happens "outside their skin", or anyway to what they cannot take directly under control), the "usual state of affairs" is *incomplete* information – that is, firms can only decide on a *limited* amount of information with respect to that "dispersed" throughout the economy.

From the standpoint of this volume, this way of examining the role of information in business behaviour has a major implication: that is, "the more stable the secondary information, ... the larger the firm can become" (Malmgren, 1961, p. 416).[19] And since secondary information becomes *less and less* stable as the level of uncertainty increases, we are to expect that in the face of rising uncertainty (rising information costs, or less information available) it will become more and more difficult for the firm to expand.

This sort of problem will be very much enhanced when the available time gets shorter, for "the imposition of a time limit means that decisions will be based on a *restricted quantity* of information, *or the firm will have to employ more specialists in information collection*" (Malmgren, 1961, p. 409, emphasis added). This last point is especially relevant, for it sheds some light upon the central role played by the *width* of the overall *amount* of information to be faced – much *more* than its *cost* – in limiting the possibility for firms to keep their environment under control.[20] The crucial issue here lies precisely in the overwhelming *scale* that the explosion of (more or less) relevant "news" has reached (often owing to the effects of new information technologies): given the time span over which they can take their decisions, firms are simply unable to process the amount of the data they receive, regardless of the *cost* of information collection.[21]

2.4.2 Then, insofar as the available time to take decisions has *actually* become shorter – because of the development of a constantly *changing* market environment – firms should have been driven to *enlarge* the number of employees involved in collecting and assessing data. The point here is that in our framework rising uncertainty is coupled with stronger levels of *competition*. That is, at the same time as firms have to deal with a more complex environment, they *also* have to *economize*.

This brings us to a question which has been at the root of the more general debate about the existence of a "managerial" limitation to the size of the firm for some considerable time. The question relates to the fact that a trade-off can be assumed as being constantly at work between the firm's capability to raise efficiency (to lower costs) and its ability to carry out its activities at a given scale. Such a trade-off stems from the existence of a basic (exogenous) constraint depending on the availability of *internal* managerial resources, which at any one time sets a structural limit to the efficiency which can be achieved in the face of the need for *constantly* adjusting to changing market conditions. The point has been paid very much attention, in particular, in the context of the problems involved by the *growth* process: both in Kaldor's (1934) and in Penrose's (1980) view (or even in the framework developed by G.B. Richardson, 1964), for example, it is assumed that firms are bounded in the possibility to (efficiently) grow by the rhythm at which they are able to develop (to "ripen") adequate *internal* managerial resources.[22]

The issue which needs to be stressed in this connection is – as was pointed out by Austin Robinson (1934 and 1935 [1931]), and later recalled in an early contribution by O. Williamson (1967) – that such a constraint acts *quite independently* of the fact that the firm is expanding its activity or not – that is, it does *not* necessarily emerge as a consequence of the growth process, but simply as a consequence of the need to keep the organization together.

As highlighted by Robinson (1934, p. 250), "Co-ordination is ... a function of the degree of change, since I myself would conceive of certain kinds of change requiring co-ordination even in a stationary state." In the words of Williamson (1967, p. 125), "customers come and go, manufacturing operations break down, distribution systems malfunction, labor and material procurements are subject to the usual vagaries, all with stochastic regularity, not to mention minor shifts in demand and similar disturbing influences of a transitory nature". A similar view can also be found in Boulding (1958, p. 72): "even on the assumption of simple homeostasis of the balance sheet, things happen to assets which are not under the direct control of the firm and therefore compel the firm to adopt a course of countervailing action. (...). An economic organization which simply sits down with a pile of assets will find, after a few years, that the assets are crumbled into decay".

All such statements refer to the point that if by any ("historical") chance things get more complex (that is, more information is required, so to speak, for any "unit of decision"), the firm *can no longer keep* the *present* scale of its operations – provided a constant efficiency level has to be maintained. Since it has to devote more resources than before to evaluating the information which is required for simply running its *current* activity, *and at the very same time* it has to reduce its overall costs, the firm is forced in this context to *reduce its own complexity*. That is, it will try to *re-equilibrate* the balance between internal managerial resources and the scale of activity *at a lower size level*.

The same question can be envisaged from the more traditional way of expressing Robinson's constraint in terms of organizational complexity, according to which the need for coordination rises *more than proportionately* as far as organizations become larger. In Robinson's own words, "a mistake made by a platoon commander demands only an instantaneous 'As you were!' A mistake by an Army Commander may require days of labour to set right. In just the same way the problem of organising a large firm grows in complication as the firm grows" (p. 41).[23]

It may be of some use at this point to stress the difference between this way of looking at the "managerial constraint" and the basically static view which characterizes the more "traditional" ways of approaching the issue, among which we may include the Neoinstitutionalist approach itself. An example of such an approach may be found in Coase's own words, when he observes that "as more transactions are organised by an entrepreneur, it would appear that the transaction would tend to be either different in kind or in different places. This furnishes an additional reason why efficiency will tend to decrease as the firms gets larger" (1937, p. 397). The point here is that the degree of efficiency of organizing transactions inside the firm is deemed to depend on some limit set by the difficulty of coordinating activities as they become more and more "scattered" on physical or merceological grounds. From this point of view it may be interesting to quote from Coase's conclusion: "changes like the telephone and the telegraph which tend to reduce the cost of organising spatially will tend to increase the size of the firm. All changes which improve managerial technique will tend to *increase* the size of the firm" (emphasis added).

Yet, what we know about the developments of the "managerial technique" over the last thirty years lead us to note that in the face of an enormous *increase* in the power to deal with organizational complexity, as has been brought about by new technologies, a general *fall* in the size of firms has occurred (see below, chapters 3 and 4). That is, as we have recalled, large firms have not simply stopped growing – they have quite substantially *shrunk*. Thus, in order to explain this point we need instead a theory which can account for the fact that in the face of rising "environmental complexity" firms – given the available resources – cannot even *maintain* the size level they had *already* achieved, even in the context of a quite relevant relaxation of any organizational constraint.

2.4.3 In the previous section we saw that the passage from "hierarchies" to the market (the expansion of inter-firm transactions) means, in structural terms, an overall increase in the *number* of "transacting" units – other things being equal, a given number of large organizations makes way for a higher number of smaller ones. And indeed, evidence seems to put in the light that a major annex of the "re-emergence of small-scale production" appears to lie just in the uprise of a strong impulse to *new* firm formation (see this volume, chapters 1 and 4).

As we have seen (above, section 2.3), a basic premise for a reorganization of business activity along such lines lies in the functioning of the market mechanism itself (be it strengthened by inter-firm cooperation or institutional enforcement of "trust" or whatever). But aside from any consideration of how efficient transacting through the market may be, a specific point in this connection is represented by what enables new (smaller) firms to cope with the task of "substituting" once and for all (larger) vertically integrated units. More precisely, the question may be put in terms of what actually enables smaller firms – at least potentially – to carry out inside *their own* skin the activities which were previously carried out within a large firm *as efficiently* as it did. In more direct terms, where do the "organizational capabilities" required for implementing such "new" task come from?

The most obvious answer is that they just come from the dis-integrated large unit itself. That is to say, "firms are brought into existence by firms". This clearly represents a quite different perspective as compared to the one which assumes firms as "naturally" originating (entering the market) by virtue of the sheer strength of some economic opportunity (mainly boiling down to positive expected profitability). In our perspective, the *preliminary* condition for a new firm to be established is given instead by the fact that a world of hierarchies did *already* exist. In other words, the very birth of smaller units is made possible by the *previous* existence of some managerial capability "dispersed through the economy", which has already been developed within *another* (larger) organization.

As suggested by Tuck (1954), any organization is in fact characterized by a given distribution of (individual) ranks, which is determined by the maximum number of immediate subordinates that a single individual can control. Yet, it may happen (and in Tuck's view it *normally* does) that – as a consequence of some process of personal advancement inside the hierarchy – at any one hierarchical level the actual number of individuals is higher than would be compatible with the "ability to control" available at the closest rank above. Therefore, a "surplus" of individuals (of capabilities) may occur. But in turn "surplus individuals are available to operate as heads of *independent* firms of ... smaller size" (p. 13, emphasis added). Such being the case, a process can be set up which leads to the reconciliation of the mentioned divergence through the emergence of "independent firms widely ranging in size".

Tuck's analysis helps to focus on a central theme in the perspective outlined above: in a world characterized by rising "environmental complexity" (that is, by rising costs of managing firms' activities *at any one hierarchical level*), it may well happen that the capabilities of each rank of controlling its immediate subordinates gets lower. This would determine at the next rank below a surplus of individuals, who may in turn be able to manage "new" organizations up to the size corresponding to the number of subordinates they were *already* in charge of controlling. The availability of the "ability to control" sets from this point of view an important premise for new "independent" firms of smaller size to be created.[24]

2.5   Searching for biological analogies

2.5.1   An extremely powerful analogy for analysing the observed changes in the growth pattern of firms can be found in the theory of growth of living organisms developed by population ecology – and, in particular, in the so-called "*r* and *K* selection" approach. From this point of view it can be observed that – broadly speaking – populations may develop according to two quite distinct evolutionary patterns, which reflect the degree of "stability" of the environment in which they live.[25]

If we define as "*r*" (the "biotic potential") the capacity of a population to increase, and as "*K*" (the "carrying capacity") the population size that an area has the resources to support, we can say that in *stable* habitats populations will spend most of their time near *K*, whereas in *unstable* habitats they will not – in particular, when conditions are favourable, they would be growing towards *K*, whilst as conditions become more unfavourable (that is *K* drops), the environment may become *overcrowded*. Such a pattern implies that, with respect to a "stable" habitat, a "fluctuating" one will lead towards higher reproductive rates, which in turn lead to smaller offspring and hence smaller adults, and will result in a greater probability of death due to environmental fluctuations.

In a very stylized form, it can therefore be said that where *K* selection is at work (in a stable environment), the overall size of the population will be steady, only a few offspring will be generated, they will become large, and they will be generally associated with a long life. Where *r* selection (a fluctuating environment) prevails, then the population itself will tend to fluctuate, and in order to compensate for higher development constraints – which involve a shorter life as well as a smaller size of organism – a much higher number of offspring will be generated.

2.5.2   There is a remarkable analogy between these two patterns of development of living organisms and the two different patterns of firms' behaviour outlined above. We can nonetheless develop a little further the analysis of how biological analogies can help us to consider the factors which affect the "passage" from large- to small-scale organizational structures. Following the work carried out by Mason Haire in the course of the 1950s (see Haire, 1959), in particular, it seems possible to find some more linkages with the perspective opened by Robinson's view.

The basic point we can start from is that the major insight stemming from the observation of the behaviour of biological organisms is to be found in the (long-run) relationship between their growth and their *shape*. Organizations, like living organisms, spend most time and effort in "holding the thing together as a single working unit" (p. 303); that is, they have to devote a given amount of their internal resources simply to *living*. This means that a larger size would bring increased pressures upon the existing structure (the "skeleton") of the organization (the organism) itself, which in turn would call for a reshaping of its internal structure, according to the principle that – as happens in living organisms – the organization is expected to become stronger where the forces tending to hamper its activity are greater.[26]

On empirical grounds, Haire observes that as an organization gets larger a rapid increase in the proportion of people allocated to administration (to *control* and *coordination*) does occur – that is, the proportion of new people absorbed by *staff* functions grows at an increasing rate, whereas the rate of growth of those absorbed by *line* functions declines.[27] This involves a significant *change* in the internal shape of the organization itself, reflecting the need to face its increasing *complexity*. Specifically, such a pattern of change suggests that coordination and control are the functions where the "disruptive" forces are focused.

But the distinction suggested by Haire between "line" and "staff" (as it relates to the changing pattern of a firm's workforce in the course of growth) also highlights a further issue in the matter; that is, what we may call "the shortsightedness" of firms' capability to think about their own development process. The point is that provided growing "risk and fluctuations" push towards *lower* organizational complexity (that is, a lower size), they also mean that in the course of downsizing (and, as also happens when companies become larger) the internal shape of the firm is likely to change.

As we have seen (section 2.3), due to the fact that a growing share of transactions (previously managed inside firms) shifts towards the market – therefore increasing the need to collect relevant information – a correspondingly growing share of the overall workforce will be involved in "line" activities, aimed at simply monitoring what is happening in the market at any one time. Given available resources, this involves in turn that the share of "staff" people – that is, those usually devoted to look at ("to *plan*") the activities of the firm in a long-run perspective – will be *reduced* accordingly. This seems to be a very effective mechanism whereby the capability of firms to deal with *more* than short-term issues becomes locked in some sort of vicious circle: the less the firm can rely upon (the ripening of) its *internal* resources to evaluate the "environmental risk", the less the very premises for future expansion can be set up, so that activities will be more and more confined within the narrower boundaries of short-term "optimal" allocation of resources.

This is one more point recalling Robinson's view about the functioning of "complex" organizations, as it relates to the distinction (referring to "line" as opposed to staff activities) "between the work of organizing *current* production and *the work of thinking ahead* and *planning* improvements in the methods of production and organisation" (1935, p. 42, emphasis added). But in an "analogical" perspective, the crucial difference between the organizational answer to "standard" market conditions, and the one which is needed when "turbulence" takes altering the logic of planning, can well be appreciated even through the words of the very father of biological analogies himself:

> *Perfectly reflex* actions ... are performed by the responsibility of the local nerve centres without any reference to the supreme central authority of the thinking power, which is supposed to reside in the cerebrum. But all *deliberate* movements require the attention of the chief *central* authority: it receives information ... and sends back detailed and complex instructions to the local authorities,... and so *co-ordinates* their action as to bring about the required results (Marshall, 1920, p. 208, emphasis added).

2.6 An overall view

2.6.1 In the last quarter of the twentieth century the macroeconomic environment in advanced countries experienced a significant break in its structural parameters. The upsurge of foreign exchange risk, sharp increases in the volatility of interest rates (including higher *real* interest rate levels), an unprecedented need to monitor rising prices and – on the market side – the joint effects of rising competition and increasingly fluctuating demand (including the fading away of mass production) have on the whole defined a "new" framework within which firms have had to set their production strategies.

These changes have made it harder to evaluate future returns to investments; at the same time they have also compelled firms to become more cautious about their involvement in non-core business activities. On the other hand, we know (as we will show in chapters 3 to 5 below) that over the same period a major change in the firm size structure has *actually* occurred, which has seen an employment shift from large-scale units towards smaller ones, involving in most cases a reduction in the average size of firms and establishments.

These two phenomena are related facets of the same long-run process of structural change. In this connection, this chapter has tried to highlight *which* theoretical framework may be addressed in order to identify the mechanisms whereby the first phenomenon has affected the second one – the starting point of the analysis being that a *single* theoretical view has to be adopted to explain firms' behaviour *both* in the course of the Golden Age *and* afterwards.

Among the few categories which the box of tools of microeconomics can make available to the economist in such a context, a few theoretical points which allow us to approach this issue have been considered here. Building in particular on the work of Malmgren, Richardson and Robinson, it seems possible to outline a framework which can help us to explain the changing logic of firms' behaviour in the passage from the Golden Age to the "new" phase of industrial development starting in the mid-1970s. We can try to summarize the view set forth above as follows:

(i) By the early 1970s, increasing financial uncertainty (the "Bretton Woods crisis" effect) meant that a larger amount of information needed to be processed by firms. According to the view set forth by Richardson (1960) and Malmgren (1961), in the face of such a change firms can *in principle* follow two distinct strategies: the first consists in keeping constant (organizational) internal requirements, leading to the processing of a *lower* proportion of relevant information than before; the second would require more resources to be allocated to "information collection". The first strategy simply means that firms, in order to take their decisions as quickly as before, have to reduce the overall amount of "external" information which is relevant for them (that is, the number of decisions to be taken); this involves a reduction in input endowments, that is decreasing firm size. The second would allow the firm to maintain the rapidity of their decisions, but – unless for some reasons firms are able to raise *exogenously* the speed of their decision-making system for any given unit of information requirements – it would also involve a larger amount of input endowments. And insofar as increasing size – following Robinson (1935) – means higher organizational complexity, this would lead to lower efficiency.[28]

(ii) The point, in this framework, is that firms also have to face the constraints imposed by competition: this means that they simply *cannot* become less efficient than before. Hence, rising competition will demand *lower* input endowments per unit of output, forcing firms to opt for the first option outlined above. Keeping efficiency (at least) constant, therefore, requires the externalization of *some* activities previously carried out by the firm inside its boundaries. This leads *in itself* to lower *fixed* costs (the firm will buy some intermediate inputs – be they goods or services – instead of making them), even if we do not take into account a second kind of uncertainty – that is, the uncertainty that arises from more volatile markets for (final) *products*. By explicitly introducing *market* uncertainty as well, we can say that firms will be pushed to reduce fixed costs (that is, to change the *composition* of total costs)[29] for one additional reason: namely, the fact that it has become increasingly difficult to *anticipate* future changes in *demand* (that is to say that for vertically integrated firms future returns are less predictable than future *costs*).

(iii) But the (historical) *fact* that rising uncertainty is coupled with rising competition leads to one more consequence: that is, the fact that firms are pushed to *select* the activities to be shed out, by concentrating themselves on the "most efficient" ones (that is, those activites in which they enjoy some comparative advantages *sub specie* of lower average costs, due to relatively higher *competencies*). This "competition" effect adds to the constraint on firms' purchases of new resources, affecting the *nature* of activities to be externalized. Externalizing (less efficient) activities means in turn that some other (possibly new) firms will take the job of producing them. The possibility for such firms to be "new" ones is enhanced by the lowering of entry barriers brought about by the choice of previously integrated firms to no longer compete in these markets.

(iv) According to this framework, the joint effects of rising financial uncertainty (which would require more resources in order to maintain previous efficiency in decision-making), rising market uncertainty (requiring lower *fixed* costs) and rising competition (requiring lower *overall* costs) push existing firms to become "less complex" (that is, smaller in size, at least as far as their input endowments are concerned), and lead new (generally small) firms to enter the market. The overall result will be a (certainly) higher *number* of small firms within the industrial system, a (possibly) lower average size in terms of input in the whole population of firms (unless the *final* market grows at a faster rate than productivity, which, as we saw in chapter 1, is not the case[30]), and *therefore* a larger share of resources (for example, employment) allocated to smaller firms (provided their productivity does not grow at a faster rate with respect to large ones). This corresponds quite closely to what the empirical analysis contained in chapters 3, 4 and 5 below will show.

2.6.2   The above stylized framework can be expressed graphically by showing the sequence of causal links leading from macroeconomic changes to structural shifts in business size. This is done in Figure 2.1, where the relation between (exogenous) macroeconomic changes[31] and (endogenous) changes in the organization of industrial activities are linked to each other.

First, let us start by considering the effects of rising uncertainty upon the amount of relevant information required to take the firm under control. Having to face the "new" situation (corresponding to the passage from u_1 to u_2 in quadrant I), in order to keep constant the speed of its response to market impulses the firm will reduce the overall amount of relevant information from i_1 to i_2 (quadrant II), and therefore – given the existence of a positive relation between speed of response and input endowments (quadrant III) – its size in terms of inputs from l_1 to l_2 (quadrant IV). Hence, the effect of rising uncertainty upon firm size will be negative.

In theory, provided there are no reasons to assume it is able to raise its "ability to process information" (which would entail a shift towards the right of the curve in quadrant II), the firm could try to meet the higher information requirements brought about by rising uncertainty (in order to keep constant its speed of decision-making) only by increasing the amount of input endowments, as is shown by the dotted curve in quadrant III. But as far as new resources are internalized by the firm, the more than proportionate rise in coordination costs involved by the Robinson constraint will, *ceteris paribus*, reduce firm efficiency from π_1 to π_2 (quadrant V). And, as we have seen, at the very same time it happens that competition is tightening, asking the firm for *higher* efficiency.[32] In this connection we can assume here competition as *given* at the level corresponding to point c^* in quadrant VI: it follows that the firm simply cannot take any more its former size, that is the size it was previously

Ir: relevant information to be processed
F: speed of information processing
L: firm size terms of input endowments
U: uncertainty
C: competition
Π: organizational efficiency
N: overall number of firms in the market

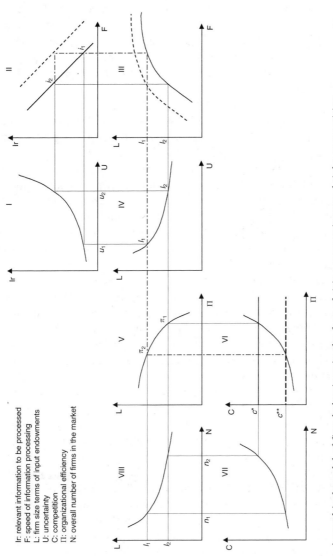

Figure 2.1 A graphical model of firm behaviour in the face of rising uncertainty and tight competition

able to manage – for this could happen only in the face of a *decrease* in competition from c^* to c^{**}.

On the other hand, as competition can be assumed to be positively correlated to the number of firms in the market (quadrant VII), the passage from u_1 to u_2 leads – given c^* – to an increase in the *number* of firms from n_1 to n_2. This involves in turn (quadrant VIII) a negative relation between firm number and size, so that the final outcome of the hypothesized changes will consist both in lower size and higher number of firms in the market.

From the point of view of the theory of the firm, this path reflects a model of firm behaviour we can broadly define as "Robinsonian", insofar as it hinges on the principle according to which the "optimal" organization of economic activities is a function of the *external* context. In this view, a crucial condition is represented by the difference between "stable" and "unstable" market environments (where stable denotes a low degree of uncertainty and competition, and unstable its opposite). Whereas in the first case the "economies of planning" overcome the advantages which may be drawn from "flexibility", in the second things work in the opposite direction: that is, lower organizational complexity is the efficient answer to "external" instability.[33] This means, more generally, that no one *single* optimal model of firms' behaviour can fit all market conditions – that is, *"optimizing" may mean setting up quite different organizations in different macroeconomic contexts.* Provided that an excess of "entrepreneurial supply" is available (so that a gradual implementation of intermediate markets can develop), *this* is the way in which transacting through the market may become an efficient solution to the "problem" of production.[34]

An interesting feature of the framework outlined above is that firms' behaviour in the face of the passage from a "stable" and "safe" environment to a turbulent and competitive one shows a remarkable similarity to that followed by living organisms in adapting to similar changes within their ecosystems. From this point of view, Robinson's (theoretical) approach to the analysis of business firms' behaviour can be viewed, by and large, as the translation into an economic framework of the "alternative" between the two evolutionary models outlined in section 2.5.1. We might say, in respect of this, that – even if they have been observed within utterly different contexts – two quite analogous phenomena have been given similar explanations on theoretical grounds.

3
Empirical Analysis I: Employment Shares and Absolute Employment Growth at the Size Level for Firms and Establishments: Six Industrial Countries in Two Different Phases of Industrial Development

3.1 The changing size pattern of business firms in industrial countries: current empirical research

3.1.1 By the end of the 1970s an increasing number of symptoms was drawing attention, in many developed countries, to the emergence of a new role for smaller firms in the production process, producing an apparent increase in their output share; it was claimed that this trend was paralleled by a corresponding decrease of the economic weight – in relative terms – of larger firms. In the early years of the following decade these signals led to some reflections about the potential role of small-scale production in the perspective of industrial development. Since the very beginning, the phenomenon was viewed in the light of its (potentially) being at the root of a broader change in production activities, grounded – via vertical dis-integration – in a gradual increase in the share of transactions among firms of different sizes, as well as the growing importance of economies of specialization as opposed to economies of large-scale production. The main question to be addressed in this context was to what extent the "new" phenomenon could be considered to reflect a permanent structural break in the organization of productive activities, to be destined to persist over time – more broadly, to represent a "historical alternative" to mass production.[1]

For many years, researches into the phenomenon were largely qualitative, so that up to the early 1980s empirical evidence consisted of little more than a series of case studies. The first attempts to set up a more general framework of the phenomenon on quantitative grounds emerged in the mid-1980s, and coincided with a wide-ranging empirical survey carried out by the OECD (1985), which for the first time provided a rough estimation of the actual weight of the small business sector in a number of industrial countries.[2] Following this first (rather preliminary) step, other institutions started developing research projects aimed at identifying the actual intensity of "the re-emergence of small-scale production" in different countries.

Particularly important in these developments was a book which gathered together the main results of an extensive research project set up by the International Institute for Labour Studies (Sengenberger *et al.*, 1990, hereafter ILO Research), which, drawing on the work of a group of scholars from a number of different countries, provided, for the first time, a substantial picture of the phenomenon across the industrialized world,[3] as well as an overall interpretive framework of its developments (more or less shaped along the lines of the analysis by Piore and Sabel, 1984). On the whole, the study reveals a general rising trend in the employment share of small manufacturing firms (those with fewer than 100 employees) since around the beginning of the 1970s; a similar trend can be observed as far as establishments are concerned. The picture was different in Germany, where the small business employment share remained broadly constant over the same period.[4]

In itself, employment shares trend says little about the actual economic importance of small businesses, for they may obviously turn upward even in the face of *a fall* in *absolute* employment. And indeed this is just what happens – according to the data – in all observed countries, with the notable exception of Japan, where they remain stable.[5] Such being the case, the question should be envisaged in terms of the employment *changes* occurring at the size level as well, in order to determine whether – even in the face of a negative balance in the employment shift from larger to smaller firms – the latter do actually succeed in raising the actual number of their employees. Yet, from this point of view ILO Research cannot give any reasonable indication; nor is it able to identify any clear trend at the sectoral level, in order to detect whether any aggregation bias is at work.

More broadly, it can be said that – notwithstanding the contributions by scholars from each of the countries under examination – on purely quantitative grounds ILO Research appears to have several methodological shortcomings, to do with the basic heterogeneity of the sources relating to different countries (and often even to a single country when moving across different points in time),[6] the inadequate sectoral breakdown, the limited width of the issues addressed in the analysis.

3.2 A survey of empirical contributions referring to single countries

3.2.1 Over time, the state of knowledge about this phenomenon has improved as the result of new contributions. However, these studies rarely extend beyond single-country contexts (for the most part confined to the industrialized world).[7] Any attempts to set up international comparisons have been very limited, and were restricted to the European area.[8] Furthermore, with regard to the six countries under examination in our work taken in isolation, the evidence seems to be far from homogeneous.

The individual country which has received the greatest attention is the United Kingdom. Since the early 1990s several contributions have provided empirical evidence about changes in business size structure.[9] Overall, these works show that in UK manufacturing the employment share of medium and small-sized firms (those with up to 200 employees) tends to rise – following a period in which it constantly fell – by and large from the late 1960s. In the 1980s, this trend reflects a substantial stability in employment for smaller firms (fewer than 100 employees) in absolute numbers, and a rise in both their output share and level.[10] This is paralleled by a decrease in employment and – to a lesser extent – output in large units (those with more than 1,000 employees). In more recent years, indeed, the picture is far from clear (especially as it relates to establishments), owing to strong jumps in the available statistical series.[11] Even more importantly, no evidence has been provided – apart from Henley (1994) – at the sectoral level, for analyses simply refer to manufacturing as a whole.

Overall, a picture emerges which shows that the economic weight of the small business sector has actually grown in recent decades (possibly even more than it happens in employment terms), after having been in decline since at least the early 1930s. As more recently stressed by Doi and Cowling (1998), the results obtained in this respect by small firms seem to reflect their taking the place of the largest ones, whose contribution to value added flows gradually shrinks. In employment terms, and considering the phenomenon in a long-run perspective (see in particular Hughes, 1993, whose analysis extends back to the 1920s), changes in the weight of small firms (those with fewer than 100 employees), firstly falling and then rising again, seem to reflect a basic *stability* in the absolute number of their employees, vis à vis the changing behaviour of large-sized businesses – firstly widening and lately sharply reducing their employment endowments. The image we can draw from such evidence is that of an industry in which the role of the small business sector hardly changes at all throughout the twentieth century: its absolute weight in terms of employment levels seems to undergo only minor fluctuations around an almost constant trend.

3.2.2 A less clear picture emerges from the empirical analyses focused on Germany, in spite of the growing attention paid to the question in recent years. On the whole, the literature on the subject[12] seems to offer no conclusive evidence. Neither the poor evidence provided by Weimer in the ILO Research study,[13] nor other later contributions succeed in measuring the actual extent of the changes occurring in the size structure over time – and anyway this is never done at the sectoral level. Overall evidence suggests a certain increase in the employment share of small establishments (those with between 1 and 50 employees) in the years following 1970 – in particular, in units with more than five employees and in the consumer goods sector. This trend follows a drop over the period 1950–70. As argued by Stockmann and Leicht (1994), however, whose estimations refer to a very long time period (starting from 1882), such a share shows very large fluctuations over the long run, so that, unlike the case in the UK, it cannot be said that the fall in the share in the course of the 1950s and the 1960s was to continue a similar trend in previous years – on the contrary, in the German case from the early 1930s to 1950 the share of firms with fewer than 50 employees in industries producing consumer goods had been increasing. In *absolute* terms, the evidence suggests that in the period from 1970 to the mid-1980s firms with between 5 and 50 employees show an increase in employment, compared to a drop below the threshold of 5 and a quite sharp contraction in firms employing more than 1,000 employees. No information relating to establishments is available.

The view emerging from the above mentioned contributions – with the notable exception of the paper by Weimer, whose conclusions appear, on the other hand, quite at odds with the evidence – boils down to a substantial scepticism as to the actual importance of the small business sector in the manufacturing sector. Whatever their absolute growth in economic weight, small firms' contribution to employment seems to remain small – on the basis of the sources used in these works, in 1987 (that is, the last year these studies refer to) firms with fewer than 50 employees accounted for 7.2 per cent of manufacturing employment; firms with less than 100 employees for 15.4 per cent.

3.2.3 The picture emerging from the very limited information about French industry (no information at all is available for years following the

ILO Research study), corresponds more closely to the British than to the German experience. Estimations provided by Didier and Malinvaud (1969) and subsequently by Didier (1982)[14] show that in a long-term perspective the employment share for larger *establishments* (those with more than 500 employees) has increased constantly since the early years of the twentieth century, with the exception of the period from 1931 to 1936, eventually coming to a halt at the beginning of the 1970s. From 1974, a reversal of the pattern occurs, and the relationship between absolute employment growth and firm size becomes negative. In the first phase employment falls in those establishments with fewer than 20 employees; beyond that threshold, employment growth is proportionate to the size level. In the second phase establishments with more than 500 employees undergo the sharpest decrease, whilst in the range between 20 and 200 employees the fall is lower, and in establishments below 20 employees the level of employment actually rises. The (heavily limited) sectoral breakdown seems to highlight that in the years after 1975 the employment fall in larger establishments is peculiarly high in industries producing intermediate goods.

The phenomenon is characterized by quite similar trends in two different periods (1931–36 and 1974–81) which broadly coincide, even with obvious differences, with deep economic crises. Didier (1982) suggests that it may be strongly affected by a structural difference, for firms of different sizes, in their ability to face "external" shocks – that is, small businesses would present an anti-cyclical behaviour, in the sense that they would play a role in offsetting the (cyclical) labour-shedding practices of large firms.[15] Such a hypothesis seems to be strengthened by the fact that in both phases – as Didier himself shows – the "artisan" firm sector is characterized throughout the 1970s by a strong expansion, *sub specie* of a rate of new firm formation constantly above the exit rate. Yet, the very short duration of the last phase included in the analysis (after 1974) suggests that we should be extremely cautious about the possible evolution of the phenomenon over the long term: to date, the available evidence does not allow any conclusive remarks.

3.2.4 In spite of being the most widely investigated country with regard to this phenomenon, Italy still has relatively few studies available in English translation. This section tries to summarize some of the findings which emerge from a large body of literature that is almost completely unknown abroad.[16] Indeed, the very issue of a changing pattern of firms' size structure in Italy has come into existence as a possible subject for empirical analysis only relatively recently: until the early 1980s – that is, until some strong signals of structural change did emerge throughout the industrial system, the general perception of a rising importance of large enterprises in manufacturing activities appeared as an obvious implication of industrial development as such, so that no special attention was paid to a phenomenon which was deemed to simply reflect the "natural" laws of industrialization. Hence, empirical analyses only started flourishing in the course of the 1980s, that is after the Industrial Census for 1981 highlighted the "re-emergence" of a large small business sector in the industrial sector, reversing the previous trend.[17]

On the whole, empirical analyses help to focus first of all on the fact that – despite an overall increase in average size of firms during the Golden Age years – at the beginning of the 1970s Italian manufacturing still appeared characterized in *structural* terms (that is, independently of *changes* in the size pattern) by a peculiarly high proportion of (very) small enterprises with respect to other developed countries. As will be clearly illustrated in the following pages, Italy shares this feature with Japan,[18] which is the other 'latecomer' *large* industrial country, having entered modern industrial development *later* than major world industrial economies. As to size trends, quantitative studies broadly agree about three main points: (i) between 1971 and 1981 employment shares rise in firms with fewer than 50 employees only, and fall in higher size classes; (ii) in the same period, however, *absolute* employment increases up to the threshold of 500 employees, and falls above this figure (this means that smaller classes do increase their employment levels in absolute numbers quite remarkably); (iii) after 1981, absolute employment rises only in those firms with fewer than 50 employees; in particular, micro-firms (those with fewer than six employees) are characterized by a different pattern with respect to small ones, that is they undergo a *decrease* in employment vis à vis the increase registered by firms included in the range within 6 and 50. Even if smaller firms, on the basis of such evidence, seem to play a positive role in sustaining industrial employment, it has to be stressed nevertheless that they do not succeed in compensating for the downward employment trend in larger ones. In this respect, the absolute loss of jobs in Italian manufacturing seems to be a structural feature of the more recent phase of industrial development as much as the increasing role of small businesses as producers.

3.2.5   For countries outside Europe the statistical evidence is no wider. For the two other large industrial economies included in this work, namely Japan and the United States, the state of knowledge goes little further than the empirical findings of the ILO Research study. In the case of Japan, in spite of the considerable interest in the phenomenon in recent years the evidence seems to indicate only marginal changes in manufacturing size structure – at least since the early 1950s. Such evidence – which, owing to very tight constraints in data collection criteria, only pertains to establishments – emerges both in Koshiro's contribution to the ILO volume[19] and in that of Sato (1989); less clear-cut indications can be drawn from the more recent paper by Doi and Cowling (1998).

In some respects, the divergence between what data actually say and the attention paid to the small business sector reflects some confusion between static and dynamic issues: the economic importance of small-scale production in Japan is indeed quite remarkable, and definitely wider than it is in the other countries analysed in this volume (excluding Italy). In 1985, according to the above mentioned studies people employed in manufacturing establishments with fewer than 100 employees made up 50 per cent of the total Japanese workforce, compared with slightly more than 30 per cent in the United Kingdom, slightly more than 20 per cent in Germany (1986), and slightly less than 30 per cent in France (c.1980)[20] and the United States. Along dynamic lines, anyway, it is possible to find some increase in the occupational weight of smaller establishments – at least, up to the beginning of the 1980s, of those with fewer than ten employees. This shift occurs at the expense of the largest units (those with more than 300 employees), whereas in other size classes employment shares remain almost unchanged.

Apart from the changes that occurred in the following years,[21] it can be said that Japanese industry shows an opposite structure, but a similar trend with respect to Germany: in the same way as in the latter the employment weight of the small business sector remains limited (with only a slight increase in the importance of smaller plants), in Japan it remains steadily high. According to the available literature – which, however, is rather scattered and only refers to aggregate figures – no major discontinuities in the size pattern seem to occur. In absolute terms (and for total manufacturing), the employment level in establishments with fewer than 100 employees rises to the end of the 1980s (even in the face of a fall in *total* employment after 1973); in the course of the following decade it starts to fall back again (even if in a limited way).

As to the United States, the enthusiasm for the "re-emergence" of small-scale business seems disproportionate to the size of the phenomenon. Available evidence (see the contribution by Piore in the ILO Research,[22] and the more recent work by Acs and Audretsch, 1993, ch. 4) does not go far beyond the assertion of a growing importance of smaller businesses for the economy *as a whole*, whereas when it comes to manufacturing evidence gets weaker (sometimes the same cannot be said about emphasis).

Limiting the observation to manufacturing, the above mentioned studies highlight a small increase in the employment shares of *establishments* with fewer than 100 employees since the beginning of the 1980s. As has been seen for other countries, this happens at the expense of the largest-sized units (those with more than 1,000 employees); in all other size bands employment shares appear basically constant over time.

The fast-rising attention for the emerging of the "size" issue is testified by the flourishing of empirical works for a growing number of industrial countries (for the most part included within the European and North American area). Among others, we can recall here contributions relating to Canada (see Baldwin, 1998), Norway (Spilling, 1998), Greece (Droucopoulos and Thomadakis, 1993) and the Netherlands (Carree and Thurik, 1991). In such a context the authors' view certainly do not always coincide each other – and, indeed, they often appear rather critical about the "optimistic" interpretation of the re-emergence of small-scale businesses.

Whereas on the whole the data recorded in such papers do confirm the existence of some changes in the employment shares advantaging smaller firms, these results cannot be taken in themselves as a positive signal: in the Canadian case, for instance, it is said that the phenomenon has resulted in lower wages and productivity levels in smaller units; and in Norway it is suggested that it simply reflects a structural weakening of large-sized enteprises, mirroring an actual decline in the industrial system.

3.3   Currently available sources for international comparisons

3.3.1   A different kind of contribution is given by other works which – even if they lack any analytical intention – may be regarded as attempts to build data-sets aimed at making international comparisons on a reasonably homogeneous data basis. In such cases information goes deeper inside manufacturing, generally offering the possibility to get a view of the phenomenon for individual industries. Moreover, information in some cases extends up to include output as well as employment levels. This category of works plays a quite relevant role – at least potentially – insofar as the above mentioned studies, generally referring to single countries, most often make it extremely difficult, not to say impossible, to make any cross-country comparisons, because they are based upon quite dissimilar sources (not always the best available).

In this context we can consider either the data-set built by Van Ark and Monnikhof (1996, hereafter vA&M) for OECD, relating to five large industrial countries, or the series of reports jointly published by Eurostat and the European Commission (DG XXIII) since 1992 (*Enterprises in Europe*, see Eurostat, various issues). The first source, even if more limited as to its country coverage, is undoubtedly the more relevant from the perspective of long-term analysis, for it tries to make available for empirical research purposes an information set for each of three different points in time (one year around the early 1970s, one year towards the end of the same decade, and one year at the beginning of the 1990s). Data are collected about firms (*or* establishment, depending on countries), employment, value added and in some cases gross output (turnover), with reference to several manufacturing industries;[23] the countries included are the same as in the ILO Research study, with the exclusion of Italy.

With relation to *Enterprises in Europe*, we have to mention that it considers many more countries, even if they are anyway by definition included within the European boundaries,[24] as well as a broader range of economic activities (all those included within the Codes 1 to 9 of the Nace 1970 classification). Apart from considerable differences in the sources employed for the various countries,[25] the main problem, in this case, is given by the absolute absence of any information for years prior to the 1990s, which makes it impossible to make use of this source for analysing the evolution of firm size structure *over the long run*.

3.3.2 In this context a singular contribution is the data-set put together by Ehrlich (1985), as the outcome of a research project developed in the first half of the 1980s at the Vienna Institute for Comparative Economic Studies. This study provides data about firm size structure for 18 countries (seven from Eastern Europe), with reference to a fairly long time period (from the beginning of 1900 up to about 1970); moreover it tries to set the analysis of the observed trends within an analytical framework.[26] Despite its limited relevance in terms of this book – the period of data collection stops at the very beginning of the 1970s, which just coincide with the outset of the "Restructuring" phase here analysed – Ehrlich's work contains very interesting information which can be compared to that emerging from above mentioned studies.

For the years prior to the Second World War, Ehrlich's data are limited to three countries (United States, Switzerland and Hungary); the evidence across these three countries seems to reveal rather similar features. First of all, data show a general trend towards the rising average size of establishments (at least when they refer to the entire size distribution, that is they include micro-units). When excluding micro-units (fewer than 5–10 employees), this trend is less clear;[27] in Hungary average size in establishments with less than ten employees falls until about the early 1920s, and rises afterwards. In the post-war years the picture appears more varied. In this case data – referring to the population of establishments with more than ten employees – again put in the light a general increase in average size, but they also show a sharp difference between Western European countries (where size increase is lower) and Eastern ones (where the increase is higher).

There appears to be some interest in the fact that in respect of "light" industries for the group of *capitalist* countries no changes at all seem to occur (compared to fairly evident upward changes of the establishment size structure in "heavy" industries, as well as in mechanical and food industries). These indications suggest that sectoral biases may play some role when simply exploring the phenomenon at the aggregate level (as is usually the case in almost all of the above mentioned studies). On the other hand, the fact that the increase in size during the years previous to Second World War (which include the Golden Age period) results higher in (then) planned economies draws in itself the attention upon the importance of organizational issues in determining the scale of manufacturing activities:[28] from this point of view, Ehrlich's data confirm that – even when the analysis relates to establishments, instead of firms – technology is by no means to be considered as the only one determinant of the size structure of an industrial system.

3.4   Some new empirical evidence: the long-run dynamics of firms' employment shares

3.4.1   In the following pages we try to provide some new evidence – with reference to major industrial countries – about the existence and the intensity of changes in firms' size structure that have occurred since the early 1960s. The aim to provide a more rigorous empirical framework reflects the point that – as emerges from our previous survey – quite often the absence of sound evidence about the "re-emergence of small-scale production" is a result of weak empirical analysis, or incomplete data-sets, or both.

Our analysis hinges upon an *ad hoc* original data-set which has been constructed around national (primary) sources. All of the characteristics of the data-set are described in Appendix A. We only recall here that it refers to those countries that were included in the ILO Research study, that data are collected with respect to *both* manufacturing firms and establishments (where available) and their employment at the 2-digit Isic (Rev.2) level, and that they refer to three different points in time (the early 1960s, the mid-1970s and the mid-1990s.[29] Size is expressed in terms of numbers of employees; a discussion about this specific point is contained in Appendix B. The need for a new data-set, apart from some major shortcomings affecting other sources either as to the completeness or the reliability of data (see Appendix A), comes from the desire to observe the phenomenon over a time span long enough to include *at least some* of the Golden Age years (the 1960s), in order to provide a measure of the differences in firm behaviour across both of the phases of industrial development dealt with in this analysis.

According to the approach followed so far, the first issue to be faced was to measure, for firms and establishments belonging to any given country, changes occurring in employment shares at the size-class level (that is, what in fact represents almost the only phenomenon taken into account in most studies devoted to the analysis of business size structure). In this connection, attention has been focused, in particular, upon the changes relative to the economic weight of smaller and larger units.

A first picture of such changes can be found in Figure 3.1, showing employment share trends for firms with more than 500 and fewer than 100 employees, respectively.[30] The distance of both thresholds from the extremes of the size distribution makes it possible to obtain a stylized picture of the phenomenon without bounding its observation to a fraction of the population: in the different countries under examination, the overall employment share included in calculations fluctuates within the range of 70 to 90 per cent of the total amount.[31]

As to this subset the figure indicates the existence, around the mid-1970s, of a watershed between a first phase in which large firms (still) "attract" employees to a greater extent than smaller ones, and a second phase witnessing a sharp decline in their importance in terms of employment. This pattern is similar – even with some differences – in the various countries. It has to be noticed that the change is most intense in Italy (that is, in the country where the weight of big business is the lowest since the very beginning of the observed period), whilst it appears almost imperceptible in Germany (where, by contrast, such weight is quite high).[32] In particular, data show a quite visible deepening of the difference between Italy and the other countries studied;

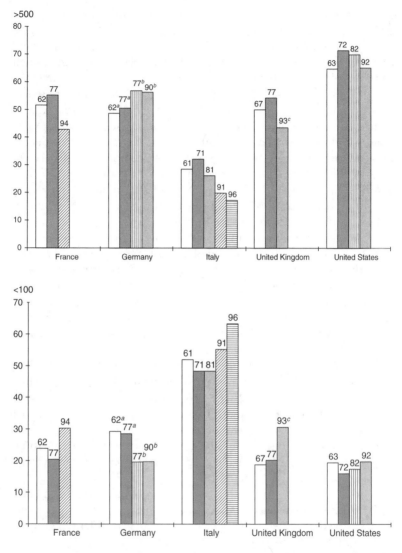

Figure 3.1   Employment shares in firms with more than 500 and fewer than 100 employees, manufacturing

[a] The smallest size class includes handicraft.
[b] The smallest size class excludes handicraft.
[c] Codes 353 and 354 excluded, codes 23 and 29.1 included (see Appendix A).

Source: See Appendix A.

this corresponds to a notable employment shift within Italian industry at the size level: in 25 years the share belonging to firms with more than 500 employees reduces to a half of its initial amount. Evidence about those firms with fewer than 100 employees seems consistent with the above data. Apart from Germany, where the changes are again quite small, the only exception is the United Kingdom, where the employment share of small firms rises since the first phase. In itself, this is not in contrast with the hypothesis that employment in *micro-units falls* anyway in the course of the Golden Age, for in this case data are available from 1968; be that as it may, since the end of that decade the inversion in the size pattern seems to have started, for small firms are already increasing their employment shares. Since employment shares have simultaneously risen in larger firms (those with more than 500 employees) as well, however, it can be said that British industry has been characterized in the years between 1968 to 1977 by some "polarization" process – that is by an employment shift towards the extremes of the size distribution.

Insofar as the observed trends may be affected by sectoral biases, a more detailed exploration has been attempted. In particular, changes occurring in the size structure have been measured by calculating, at each point in time, the ratio of the employment share of small firms (below 100 employees) to the share of large ones (above 500). Figure 3.2 shows the relative values of such ratios, with the level assumed by the ratio at the beginning of each period set at 100.[33] Comparisons among the various pairs of figures highlight the point that (relative) employment shifts can be observed across almost the entire range of industries in most countries. For the most part, in the Golden Age bars measuring the weight of small firms relative to large appear below the straight line showing the initial value of the index, whereas in the subsequent phase they appear above. Again, Germany is an exception (this means that the stability in the German shares revealed by Figure 3.1 above reflects different trends in different industries).

3.5   The long-run evolution of employment shares at the establishment level

3.5.1   A more complete picture can be obtained by reapplying calculations at the establishment level (where possible). In this case (Figure 3.3) the first thing that can be observed is that, in contrast to what we have seen about firms, employment shares – with the notable

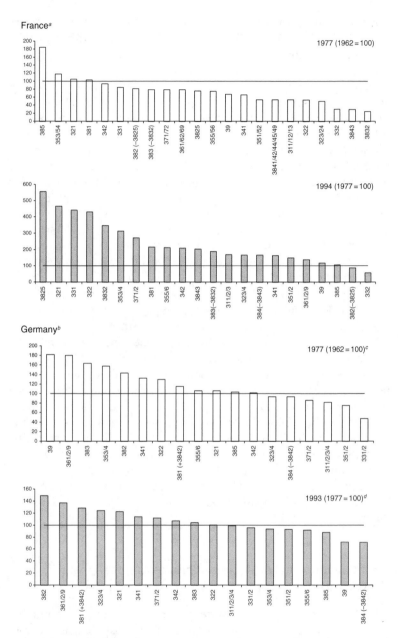

Figure 3.2 Employment shares ratio between firms with fewer than 100 and more than 500 employees, sectoral values

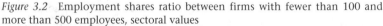

[a] Size class 0–9 and code 314 excluded (see Appendix A).
[b] Code 3842 incuded in code 381 (see Appendix A).
[c] The smallest size class includes handicraft.
[d] The smallest size class excludes handicraft.

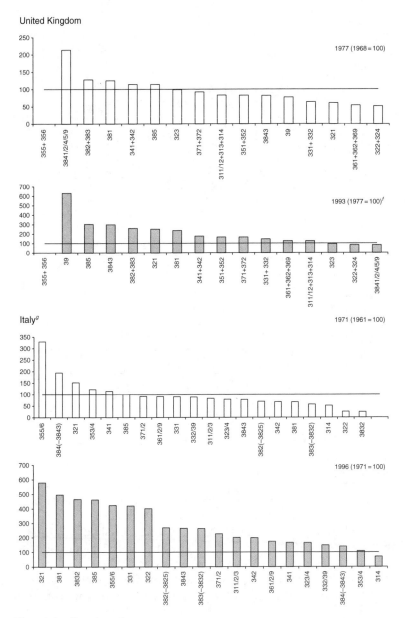

Figure 3.2 (Continued)

e Codes 353 and 354 excluded, codes 23 and 29.1 included in 1994 (see Appendix A).

f The denominator of code 323 includes all firms with more than 100 employees.

g Codes 3825, 351 and 352 excluded (see Appendix A).

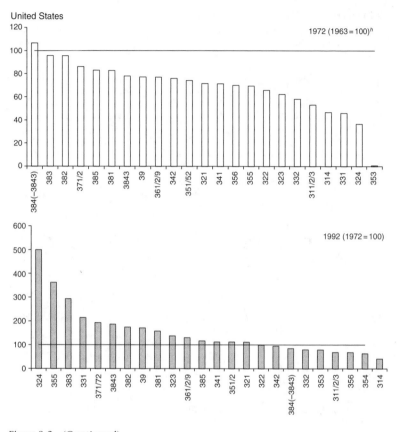

Figure 3.2   (Continued)

[h] Code 354 excluded.

Source: See Appendix A.

exception of Italy – do not show any discernible trend. In the first phase large establishments' shares are already falling in three out of five countries, and among small units the trend is towards stability (in the UK shares seem to rise). In the second phase large units' shares fall in all countries (in this case the trend is the same as for firms), but in the case of small units the picture is far less clear: in particular, shares relative to Germany and Japan do not change, those relative to other countries increase.

When comparing firm and establishment data we can observe, in particular, a noticeable difference in the relative position of Germany and the United States as to the relative proportion of larger units

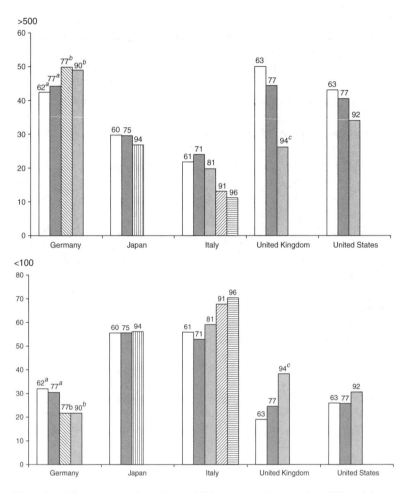

Figure 3.3 Employment shares in establishments with more than 500 and fewer than 100 employees, manufacturing

[a] the smallest size class includes handicraft.
[b] the smallest size class excludes handicraft.
[c] codes 353 and 354 excluded, codes 23 and 29.1 included (see Appendix A).

Source: See Appendix A.

(see Figure 3.1a): it might be inferred from these data that in the United States the importance of large multi-plant firms is greater (and this is certainly the case anyway),[34] but most probably the results also have something to do with differences in the very definition of the "firm" adopted in the two contexts (the definition being broader in the US case).[35]

3.5.2 Changes affecting the size distribution of establishments can be considered in greater detail by looking at the long-run evolution of cumulative employment shares (see Figure 3.4). This way of analysing data allows us to identify at the beginning of the period under examination a polarization, across countries, of the size pattern, reflecting the time sequence of the industrialization process in different economies: in the 1960s Italy and Japan (the two 'latecomers') appear on the one side and Germany, the United Kingdom and the United States on the other.[36] In the first two countries almost 50 per cent of total employment is concentrated in units with fewer than 50 employees, while in other countries in order to get the same amount it is necessary to include establishments up to 500 employees. In this context, a process of convergence occurs from the 1970s in the UK pattern towards Italy and Japan: the curve relative to the UK moves upward, reaching an intermediate point between these countries on the one side and Germany and the US on the other. A more marked distance between the US curve and the German one can also be observed – the former also moving upward, even if less sharply than in the UK. On the whole, however, the distance between the two groups remains quite visible over time, consistent with what we saw in previous Figures: curves relative to the US, Germany and Japan hardly move at all; as to Italy, the

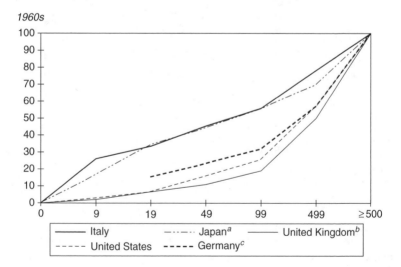

Figure 3.4 Percentage cumulative shares of employment in manufacturing establishments

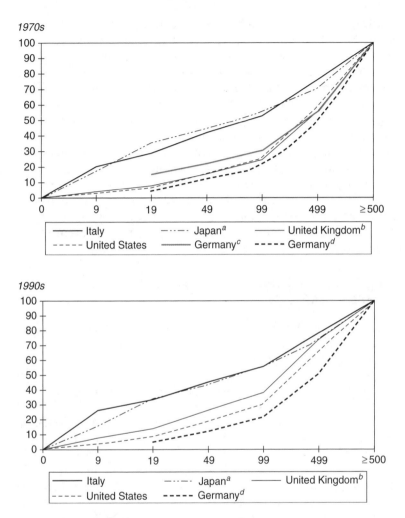

Figure 3.4 (Continued)

[a] Size classes: 1–9, 10–29, 30–49, 50–99, 100–299, ≥300.

[b] The smallest size class: 1–10; code 23 included; codes 353 and 354 excluded in 1994 (see Appendix A).

[c] The size class 1–19 includes handicraft.

[d] The size class 1–19 excludes handicraft.

Source: See Appendix A.

convergence process which seems to emerge in the mid-1970s (in particular, as it concerns size classes between 20 and 100 employees) gives way to a new trend seeing an employment shift towards smaller units. As for firms, a more dis-aggregated inspection of data does not reveal remarkable biases.[37] Table 3.1 shows that, starting at the beginning of the 1970s, the downsizing of large establishments – consistent with Figure 3.2 – extends to almost all industries (with a few exceptions in Germany); at the same time small units' shares rise almost everywhere (with some more exceptions in the case of Germany and also in the case of Japan). In these two countries – where minor downsizing effects at the aggregate level can be observed – wider divergences in sectoral behaviour occur. In such cases it can be said that different sectoral trends offset each other when considering aggregate figures, or, in other words, that aggregate figures hide the existence of some changes in specific industries.

3.6   Absolute employment changes in firms and establishments

3.6.1   Properly, as already stressed (see section 3.1), employment shares' dynamics gives no information about changes in the *number* of employees belonging to a given size class of firms (establishments). In itself the employment shift towards lower classes, from this point of view, might involve little more than a higher inertia of smaller units with respect to a downsizing process affecting – to a broader or lesser extent – the *whole* range of sizes. Were this the case, the re-emergence of small-scale production would only reflect a difference in the degree of *intensity* (a lower one) of the *same* phenomenon – no differences in *sign* being evident.

Therefore, it seems necessary to approach the question as to what happens to employment levels in absolute numbers. In this respect, an overall picture is offered by Figures 3.5 and 3.6. It can be seen clearly that both the rise (first) and then the fall in large firms' employment are evident in absolute terms as well. Similar to the evidence on shares, Germany is again an exception (absolute levels fall to 1977 and do not show any remarkable change afterwards). Thresholds differ anyway across countries: in the US and the UK the phenomenon seems to characterize firms with more than 500 employees only, whilst in France and Italy the size limit is lower (100 and 50 employees, respectively). In lower classes changes appear rather small, in both periods.

Hence, employment shifts across size revealed by changes in shares appear as the result of basically asymmetrical behaviour of large and

Table 3.1 Employment shares in establishments with more than 500 and fewer than 100 employees, nearly 1970 = 100

Isic codes	Germany 1990	Italy 1996	Japan 1994	United Kingdom[a] 1994	United States 1992
>500					
311/12 + 313 + 314	97	58	113	72	127
321	92	19	61	38	84
322 + 323 + 324	123	37	55	71	103
331 + 332	101	76	72	46	99
341 + 342	86	47	81	48	85
351 + 352	99	53	43	73	89
353 + 354 + 355 + 356	98	37	43	27	63
361 + 362 + 369	90	58	81	45	62
371 + 372	68	64	75	72	70
381	91	37	91	33	60
382 + 383	94	47	96	56	71
384	105[b]	77	92	84	94
385	89	37	87	35	97
39	127	63	94	8	69
<100					
311/12 + 313 + 314	90	113	90	142	85
321	106	145	108	163	119
322 + 323 + 324	101	126	105	105	111
331 + 332	96	100	101	115	99
341 + 342	109	127	104	149	114
351 + 352	92	153	155	157	117
353 + 354 + 355 + 356	98	149	155	203	121
361 + 362 + 369	101	117	108	169	128
371 + 372	257	165	142	147	152
381	108	113	101	132	132
382 + 383	120	156	101	167	146
384	73[b]	175	104	164	120
385	99	148	122	177	103
39	93	105	105	282	121

[a] 1994 includes codes 23 and 29.1 (see Appendix A).
[b] excluding 3842 (included in 381).

Source: See Appendix A.

small firms: in both phases, shares' changes simply reflect what happens to larger units (which first expand their employment endowments, and subsequently undergo a decline). In smaller firms, by contrast, absolute employment remains almost constant over time, showing only minor fluctuations. Viewed from the point of view of the contribution given to

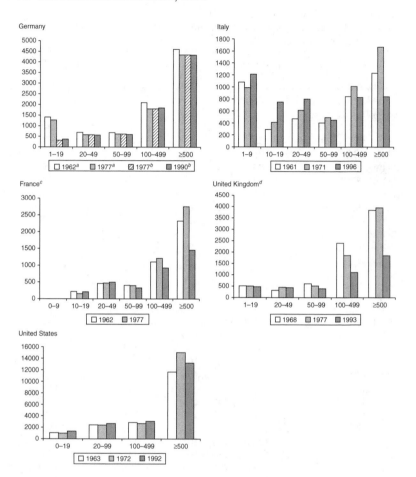

Figure 3.5   Number of employees by size class in manufacturing firms (thousands)

[a] The smallest size class includes handicraft.

[b] The smallest size class excludes handicraft.

[c] Code 314 excluded (see Appendix A).

[d] In 1968 the first two size classes are: 1–24, 25–50; codes 353 and 354 excluded; codes 23 and 29.1 included in 1994 (see Appendix A).

Source: See Appendix A.

manufacturing employment, our data reveal that *structural* change largely appears as a big business question: absolute employment changes simply bypass the small business sector, which in this context plays an essentially "passive" role. In this connection, Italy stands apart from the group: from 1971 employment grows quite strongly in firms up to the threshold corresponding to 50 employees; in this case, a real shift across size seems actually to be at work.

3.6.2   When considering establishments (Figure 3.6), no major differences arise with respect to firms with reference to both Germany and

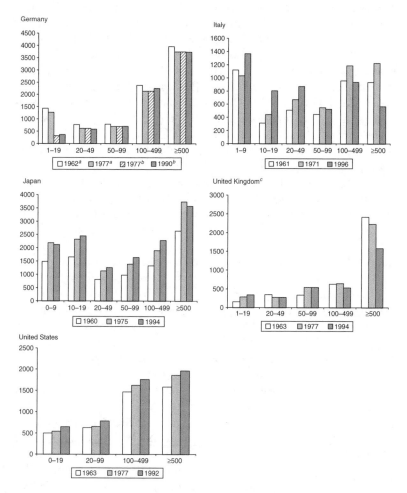

Figure 3.6   Number of employees by size class in manufacturing establishments
[a] The smallest size class includes handicraft.
[b] The smallest size class excludes handicraft.
[c] Code 314 excluded; codes 353 and 354 excluded; codes 23 and 29.1 included in 1994 (see Appendix A).
Source: See Appendix A.

Italy, whereas some differences can be observed in the cases of the UK and the US. In particular, in the UK downsizing appears to be far less marked in establishments as against firms for units above 500 employees; in the US changes in establishments with between 100 and 500 employees are relatively wider than is the case for firms in both phases.

More discernible patterns can be found in Japanese data (even if in this case, unfortunately, no comparison at all with firms can be made), which in the face of an almost absolute stability of shares in small plants show relevant changes in absolute figures. On the whole, the Japanese economy is characterized as to large units by the same trend as other industrial economies (even if the fall in employment shares after 1975 is less evident). But it also shows a remarkable difference with such countries, as far as between 1960 and 1975 it is characterized by a strong increase in employment in all *other* size classes as well – and, in particular, in small firms. Such an increase, which is larger than that which occurs in other countries, indicates a substantial stability in shares among size classes. In the following period the share of small units (plants with fewer than 100 employees) does not change, owing to a slight fall in micro-units (fewer than 10); the (limited) fall in large units' share reflects the absolute decrease in number of their employees.

3.6.3 The whole phenomenon can be stylized more clearly by putting together data relative to smaller size classes, in order to focus attention on the lower and upper portions of the size distribution (in the same way as for Figures 3.1 and 3.2). Data refer to firms (establishments for Japan); in order to make the relative trends in employment clearer, percentage employment changes with respect to initial values in each of the two periods under observation are calculated (Figure 3.7).[38] The figure shows that from the second half of the 1970s to the first half of the 1990s – excluding Germany and Japan, which do not undergo any important changes at to their employment *shares* – the negative contribution of large firms to *absolute* employment change[39] is only partially offset by the increase in employment in small firms. In four out of six countries, smaller businesses succeed in catching little more than a fraction of employees shed by large ones (in the UK not even that).[40]

Broadly speaking, the behaviour of Germany and Japan is the same as is seen for other countries (employment falls in large units and rises in smaller ones): simply, the former variation is lower than the latter in absolute terms – and it is also lower than in other countries. Large firms' behaviour, then, is decisive: in those countries where their size shrinks, overall manufacturing employment falls.

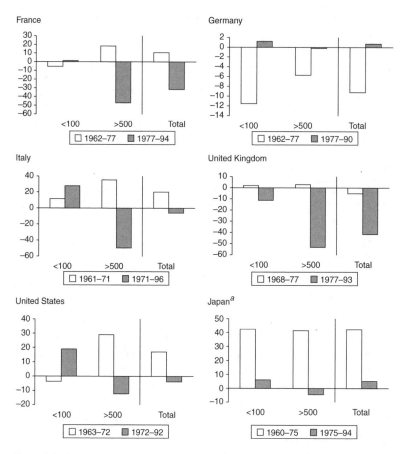

Figure 3.7 Percentage variation of employment in firms, manufacturing
[a] Data refer to establishments.

Source: See Appendix A.

The picture is less clear for the earlier phase (the Golden Age years). Here an expansion in the absolute size of the small business sector of Italy and Japan stands out since the 1960s, in contrast to the trends in other countries. Key to this phenomenon is the 'lag' in the industrialization process of both countries with respect to the other economies considered in our analysis, which brings about an increase in employment even in industries where the average size is small. In the UK the absolute fall in employment between 1968 and 1977 depends instead on firms belonging to the size range excluded from the figure (where absolute employment evidently shrinks).[41]

Table 3.2   Employment changes in firms with fewer than 100 and more than 500 employees[a]

Countries	1970s				1990s			
	<100		>500		<100		>500	
	yes	no	yes	no	yes	no	yes	no
France	12	10	16	6	10	12	19	3
Germany	11	7	12	6	6	12	11	7
Italy	17	5	17	5	16	6	17	5
Japan[b]	16	0	15[c]	1[c]	10	6	13[c]	3[c]
United Kingdom	7	10	10[d]	6[d]	10[e]	6[e]	15[e]	1[e]
United States	14	10	23	1	14	10	14	10

[a] number of sectors where employment changes show the same sign as manufacturing average.
[b] establishments.
[c] >300.
[d] excludes code 323 (value equal to zero for firms with more than 500 employees).
[e] excludes code 353 (n.a. in 1994).
Source: See Appendix A.

Sectoral data show a basic absence of relevant biases: from Table 3.2, which illustrates the frequency of cases (industries) in which employment changes assume the same sign as for total manufacturing, it can be inferred that for firms of both size groups positive values (concordance) do prevail.

3.7   Conclusions

The empirical analysis carried out in this chapter on a new data-set basis allows us to provide an overall picture of the changes in size structure which have taken place in industrialized countries since the early 1960s. Our exploration shows that over the course of the last quarter of the twentieth century a fall in the share of employment belonging to large firms occurred, paralleled by a more or less corresponding increase in the shares of small firms. This trend is counter to that which characterized the Golden Age years (from the early 1960s). From this point of view the 1970s actually represent a watershed between two quite different phases of industrial development. This phenomenon is common to almost all industrial countries, but it exhibits important cross-country differences: it seems to characterize two of the observed countries (namely Germany and Japan) to only a limited extent, whilst it is especially intense in the

Italian case – that is, in the country where the economic weight of small businesses has been peculiarly high since the very beginning of the period under examination.

The rise and fall of employment shares in large businesses occur in absolute terms as well, but this is not the same for firms in the small business sector. Employment variations show, in fact, that the absolute employment shift is basically asymmetrical: the number of employees actually moves (first upward and then downward) only in large firms, whereas it shows only minor fluctuations in small ones. Hence, small firms play a substantially *passive* role in sustaining employment levels – that is, their behaviour simply mirrors what happens in large organizations. Even in this connection the result from Italy stands out: in particular, the number of employees in firms with fewer than 50 employees increases since 1971 in *absolute* as well as relative terms.

A rather different pattern arises from data referring to establishments. In this case, even if the data show some broad similarities (especially as they refer to smaller classes, where firm and establishment often simply coincide), no definite trends can be observed at the size level as to both employment shares and absolute employment growth. In the case of Japan (where no data about firms are available), we have shown that the observed stability in employment shares at the size-class level hide an increase in absolute employment in *all* firms with more than ten employees.

4
Empirical Analysis II: The Number of Business Units and their Average Size over the Long Run: Models of Industrial Development

4.1 The determinants of industrial employment: firms' average size and number

4.1.1 The empirical evidence provided in chapter 3 shows that in the last quarter of the twentieth century industrialized countries witnessed a shift in manufacturing employment towards smaller business units. This took place – albeit to different extents – in almost all countries in *relative* terms, but it also coincided with shifts in *absolute* numbers in only two of the six countries included in the analysis – namely, Italy and Japan, that is the two 'late comer' industrial economies. This overall tendency represents a sharp reversal of the trend experienced by *all* countries since (at least) the end of the Second World War, which consisted of a constant growth of absolute employment levels in large firms (a development that is far less evident, as we have seen, as far as establishments are concerned). In (relatively) older industrial countries, then, changes in the shape of the business size distribution were basically driven by the downsizing of large firms, vis à vis a substantial *stability* in the number of employees in smaller ones. Such being the case, the observed shifts in overall employment mainly represent the outcome of the changing behaviour of *larger* units – that is, the reduction (at least in terms of the number of employees) in their average size.

In this chapter we will try to probe a little further into this issue, by assessing the existence of different patterns of industrial development in the course of the post-war period. This will help us to clarify some important differences in the nature of the different trends which can be observed when looking at different countries.

4.1.2 Long-run changes in the business size distribution of employment – in both relative and absolute terms – depend upon two different causes. The first is changes in the average size of *existing* units (hereafter firms); the second relates to changes in their *number*. Dividing firms' distribution into size classes, we can say that the former corresponds to the outcome, at the aggregate level, of the transition across size classes (employment growth) of single surviving firms;[1] the latter depends on the changes affecting, over the period involved, the very boundaries of the population itself – namely, entries of new firms ("births") and exits of existing firms ("deaths") in each size class.

Indeed, the currently available data generally make it quite difficult to observe both phenomena. In fact, time comparisons of firms' size structures – restricted to the analysis of stock data – merely show, for each of the above mentioned phenomena, the net effect (the overall balance) of long-run trends. On the one hand, we can observe changes in the average size (that is, average growth) of the firms belonging to a given size class, irrespective of their being just the same ones both at the beginning and the end of the observed period. On the other, we can get from stock data some measure of the net changes occurred in the overall number of firms, but we are not able at all to put these down to any changes either in entries (new firm formation) or in exits (failure of existing firms).[2]

Nevertheless, the relative trend in average size as against the overall number of the observed firms can help us to infer some quite interesting aspects of the industrial development pattern in different countries and periods. Assuming that $L = (L/N)N$, where L is employment and N the total number of firms, we can say that – taken to the extreme – L may change over a given time period either without any changes in average size (this happens when changes in L derive only from positive values of the net balance between entries and exits), or, at the opposite, in the absence of any changes in the overall number of firms (corresponding to positive values of firms' growth in terms of employment, which involve higher average size).

In other words, a first pattern can be identified when the expansion of the industrial system (in terms of employment) takes place mainly through a long-run upward trend in the average size of its business units; a different one is at work when the main driving force is given instead by an overall (net) addition of such units to the previous stock. Similarly, two patterns can be identified when the overall tendency of the industrial system is towards (employment) *shrinkage* – in such case the two different patterns are either downsizing or a narrowing of the stock of business units.

This is obviously true both at the aggregate level and with reference to any single size "group"; from the second point of view, in particular, the main question lies in detecting how much – in different countries and time periods – employment trends depend, in each size class, on changes in average size rather than on changes in the number of business units. Sections 4.2 and 4.3 cast a first glance, at the sectoral level and without any reference to individual size-class behaviour, to the long-run dynamics of average size (both for firms and establishments) and to the growth in the number of business units, respectively. Section 4.4 extends the analysis by measuring the relative effects on employment of average size and net-entry trends, both at the aggregate and the size-class level.

4.2   The average size of firms and establishments over the long run at the aggregate level

4.2.1   As a first issue, we can look at the long-run trend of average size – both for firms and establishments – for the manufacturing sector as a whole.[3] As shown in Table 4.1, with the exception of the United Kingdom the average size of firms rises in all countries in the course of the first phase under examination (the Golden Age), and falls in the subsequent one. The overall reduction in size since the mid-1970s appears greatest where the shifts in employment shares (as has been observed in chapter 3 above) are more pronounced – namely, in France, Italy, and the United Kingdom. When excluding units with fewer than ten employees no major differences in data seem to appear: a partial exception to this pattern, again, is Italy, where size fell even during the Golden Age period. This points to a particular role played by micro-units in affecting average size, consisting in their sharp reduction in number between 1961 and 1971 (see section 4.3 below).

As far as establishments are concerned (Table 4.2), a more variegated pattern arises from the figures. First of all, we can see a striking stability in the average size of plants in Japan: over a thirty-year period almost no changes can be found in data (and since the mid-1970s no changes *at all*), even when calculations are repeated to exclude very small units.[4] A similar pattern (slightly less static when only plants with more than ten employees are considered) emerges with reference to the United States. Moreover, a difference can be found in data referring to Germany when excluding smallest units – that is, those units with less than 20 employees (in which case after the mid-1970s average size rises instead of falling).

An opposite trend with respect to that observed for Italian firms in the Golden Age is at work here: a remarkable increase in the average size of

Table 4.1 Cross-country comparisons of average size of firms[a] (values in brackets exclude firms with fewer than 10 employees)

Years	United Kingdom		France[f]	United States		Germany[c]		Italy	
						handicraft included	handicraft excluded		
Early 1960s	92	(230)[b]	— (105)	74	—	21	—	8	(71)
Early 1970s	—	—	—	89	(182)	—	—	11	(65)
Mid 1970s	66	(204)[c,d]	— (132)	—	—	30	92 (208)	—	—
Early 1980s	—	—	—	82	(166)	—	—	10	(41)
Early 1990s	32	(143)[c,d,e]	— (84)	66	(148)	—	84 (205)	9	(39)

[a] United Kingdom: 1968, 1977, 1993; France: 1962, 1977, 1994; United States: 1963, 1972, 1982, 1992; Germany: 1962, 1977, 1990; Italy: 1961, 1971, 1981, 1996.
[b] values in brackets exclude firms with less than 24 employees.
[c] values in brackets exclude firms with less than 19 employees.
[d] codes 353 and 354 are excluded (see Appendix A).
[e] codes 23 and 29.1 are included (see Appendix A).
[f] code 314 is excluded.

Source: See Appendix A.

Table 4.2 Cross-country comparisons of average size of establishments[a] (values in brackets exclude plants with fewer than 10 employees)

Years	United Kingdom[b]		Japan[c]		United States		Germany[d]		Italy	
							handicraft included	handicraft excluded		
Early 1960s	94	(146)	18	(52)	55	(108)	21	—	8	(64)
Early 1970s	—	—	—	—	52	(110)	—	—	10	(58)
Mid 1970s	60	(119)	16	(51)	—	—	29	82 (166)	—	—
Early 1980s	—	—	—	—	—	—	—	—	9	(46)
Early 1990s	24	(75)[e]	16	(50)	52	(103)	—	78 (178)	8	(36)

[a] United Kingdom: 1963, 1977, 1994; Japan: 1960, 1975, 1994; United States: 1963, 1977, 1992; Germany: 1962, 1977, 1991; Italy: 1961, 1971, 1981, 1996.
[b] codes 353 and 354 are excluded (see Appendix A).
[c] codes 311/2/3/4 are excluded.
[d] values in brackets exclude plants with less than 19 employees.
[e] codes 323 and 329 are included (see Appendix A).

Source: See Appendix A.

very small plants seems to have occurred, whereas beyond the 20-employees' threshold the average size has dropped slightly. On the whole, with the exception of UK figures (which deserve in themselves some more attention as to the basic reliability of statistics pertaining to smaller units, be they firms or plants[5]), it can be said that in the observed countries the average size of "technical" units – as we can term plants – shows no major upward or downward trends in the course of the two phases of industrial development.

4.2.2 Whilst a closer examination of the differences in the behaviour of firms as opposed to plants will be given in chapter 5, in this section some more information is provided about the sectoral pattern of the observed trends. In such respect Figures 4.1 and 4.2 (referring to firms and establishments, respectively) show with reference to each country – on log-scale – the graphical dispersion of the sectoral values of average size at different dates (as usual, the early 1960s, the mid-1970s and the early 1990s).[6]

As far as firms are concerned, the location of single sectors on the graph, with the exception of the UK case (which show a falling average size of firms even during the Golden Age), reflects closely the general trend revealed by the aggregate figures: in most cases, the average size of firms rises in the first period, and falls in the second. With regard to the 1960s, however, it can be noticed that in the case of Italian industry sectoral trends show remarkable differences – in more than half of the observed industries average size falls, vis à vis an overall tendency to rise at the aggregate level.

These data reflect a peculiar feature (an "anomaly") with regard to Italy, which is that even during the Golden Age in some industries a tendency towards a low-scale production model – hinging upon economies of specialization as opposed to economies of large-scale production – did prevail.[7] This seems consistent with the picture emerging from Table 4.1 above, which (implicitly) shows for the whole manufacturing sector a fall in the average size of firms with more than ten employees during the Golden Age.[8]

When considering establishment data, a slightly different pattern can be identified, which provides some more elements for evaluating the differences revealed by aggregate figures in Tables 4.1 and 4.2 above. In order to make clearer the observed trends, in Table 4.3 a synoptical picture is provided which summarizes the data contained in Figures 4.1 and 4.2, by computing the share of industries showing an increase in the average size of their business units (be they firms or plants) with respect to the starting date of each period.

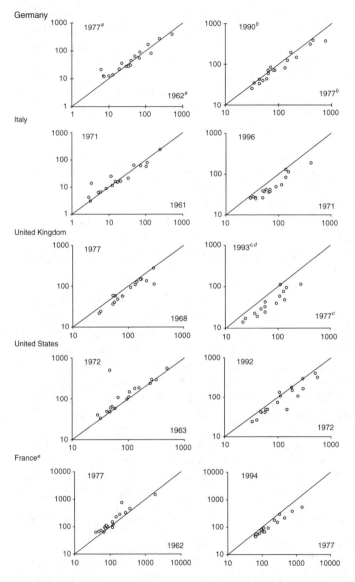

Figure 4.1   Average size of firms, sectoral values (log scale)

[a] the smallest size class includes handicraft.
[b] the smallest size class excludes handicraft.
[c] excludes codes 353 and 354 (see Appendix A).
[d] 1993 includes codes 23 and 29.1 (see Appendix A).
[e] excludes size class 0–9 and code 314 (see Appendix A).

Source: See Appendix A.

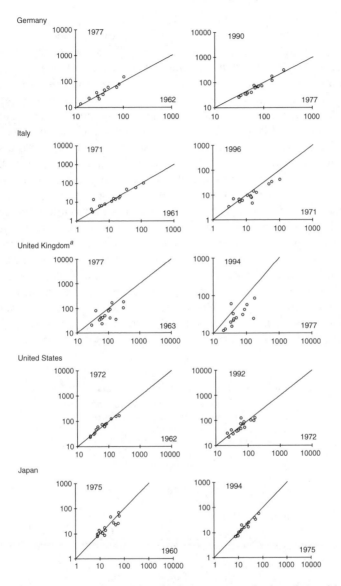

Figure 4.2   Average size of establishments, sectoral values (log scale)
[a] codes 353 and 354 excluded; 1994 includes codes 23 and 29.1 (see Appendix A).
Source: See Appendix A.

In Table 4.3, a quite different behaviour of plants as opposed to firms can first be observed in the United States. In this case, it appears at first sight that, in most industries, the average plant size shows no tendency to increase either in the course of the Golden Age or afterwards (the share of industries characterized by an increase in size is just the same in both periods). A rather low propensity to rising average size over the Golden Age can also be observed for Japan (although no information at all is available about Japanese enterprises). In Japan, the share of industries characterized by an increase in plant size produces similar results to Italy (it is identical in the Golden Age period, and lower afterwards), therefore showing that even in two late-industrializing countries – up to the early 1960s – in many industries no need at all for increasing the size of technical units was felt, even in the course of what has undoubtedly to be considered an industrialization phase.[9] Overall (no data about establishment are available in turn for France), it appears that in just one country (out of five), namely Germany, did a rise in average plant size prevail during the Golden Age.

The implications of the differences in behaviour between firms and plants will be discussed in some detail in the following chapter; we can nonetheless observe in this connection that, overall, the "rise phase" in the average size of the former (let us say the years spanning from the

Table 4.3 Synopsis of the values plotted in Figures 4.1 and 4.2: industries showing values above the initial one as a share of total industries

Countries	1st phase	2nd phase
Firms		
France	78	0
Germany	67	17
Italy	44	17
United Kingdom	6	6
United States	83	11
Establishments		
Germany	67	20
Italy	47	20
Japan	47	7
United Kingdom	13	7
United States	33	33

Source: See Appendix A.

early 1960s to the mid-1970s, provided no evidence is available for previous years) does not *necessarily* coincide in time in every country with a similar rise in the size of the latter. Indeed, with regard to technical units the Golden Age does not seem to have advanced any *compelling* reasons for their size to expand.

With regard to the following phase, it can be said that the share of industries characterized by falling average size of their establishments is always higher than the share of industries in which size increases; nevertheless, it can be noticed that, for all countries, the latter appears in turn higher than the corresponding share for firms (see the second column in Table 4.3). That is, industries experiencing a *fall* in the size of plants in more recent years are less numerous than industries experiencing a fall in the size of firms.

4.2.3 A final remark has still to be made about the possibility that in an international perspective the average sizes of technical units (establishments) may, over the long run, show a tendency to converge at the sectoral level, as the result of the diffusion across the industrialized world of similar techniques (as well as similar technologies). Had a "microelectronics effect" (leading to smaller-scale production) actually spread across all countries over the last phase of the industrial development (as is claimed in much current literature, see chapter 1) such a tendency would have been further enhanced, so that the observed fall in the average scale of plants should have been paralleled by an overall decrease of their variance within each industry. Indeed, from this point of view, it can readily be seen from the evidence provided in Figure 4.3 that the cross-country variance (relative standard deviation) of sectoral average size of plants is characterized by a remarkable tendency to *increase*.[10] This means that the net balance of the changes occurring over the two phases under examination is, if any, an overall *divergence* of "technical" (average) size structures in different countries.[11] As to the ways of organizing productive activities, some differences in "national" industrialization models seem to be at work.

4.3 The number of firms and establishments over the long run at the aggregate level

4.3.1 As has been stated in section 4.1 above, a relevant question to be dealt with in exploring to what extent different industrialization models can be identified consists in analysing, at the country level, the pattern of change in the number of business units over time. But an answer has

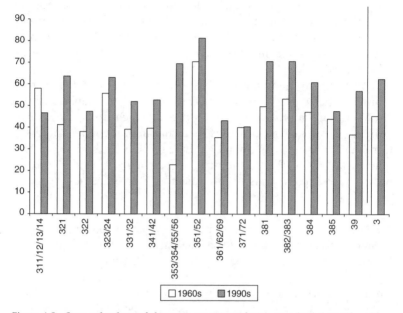

Figure 4.3   Sectoral values of the cross-country relative standard deviations for average size of establishments (units with more than 10 employees)

Source: See Appendix A.

also still to be given – on such grounds – to the hypothesis formulated in chapter 1 as to the existence of a *general* structural break in the long-run rhythm of growth in the number of firms, which – as we said there – should have characterized the two different phases of development hitherto considered.

From this point of view, it seems worthwhile to start with the second issue. As Figure 4.4 illustrates, empirical evidence clearly shows in this respect that the overall pattern stylized in chapter 1 (in which only data about "independent" *employees* for the whole manufacturing sector were analysed) perfectly corresponds, at the aggregate level, to the actual data available for firms.[12] The number of manufacturing enterprises shrinks in all countries in the course of the Golden Age (in spite of the fact that over the same period such countries are involved in a process of global expansion of their manufacturing capacity), and rises in the subsequent phase (which is, on the contrary, characterized by a general trend towards de-industrialization, at least in terms of manufacturing employment in absolute numbers – see section 4.4 below).

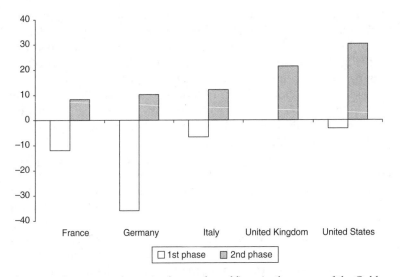

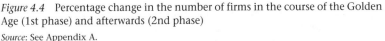

Figure 4.4 Percentage change in the number of firms in the course of the Golden Age (1st phase) and afterwards (2nd phase)

Source: See Appendix A.

Therefore, the structural break emerging in the size pattern of firms in the face of the end of the Golden Age (consisting in both a rise in the employment share of the smallest units and in a fall in the average size of all units) coincides with a general passage from negative to positive net entry rates. This means that – at the manufacturing level and for all countries – the re-emergence of an important role of small businesses after the mid-1970s hinges upon a reversal of the model inherited from the Golden Age as to the way of expanding industrial capacity.

Such a phenomenon has to be considered even more significant in the light of the fact that the entire process takes place in the face of a major discontinuity in the rate of growth of the manufacturing sector. That is, during the course of the Golden Age forces tending to *aggregate* business units were stronger than the rhythm of new firm formation driven by the very expansion in the size of the manufacturing sector itself. In the next period, forces tending to *divide* business units become stronger than the (negative) effect on new firm formation due to the overall shrinkage in the (employment) size of the manufacturing sector as a whole.[13]

4.3.2 It might be argued that the observed phenomenon should be analysed at a more dis-aggregated level, in order to detect possible sectoral biases. This is exactly what the data in Table 4.4 – referring to sectoral trends – try to highlight.[14] Yet, before considering these data, it has to be noticed that insofar as *absolute* numbers are concerned, net entries at the industry level are affected in different countries – other than by the "structural" factors so far outlined – by underlying long-run changes in the sectoral pattern of industrial activities. That is, it may happen that firm *net* entries in a given industry within a given country show, say, *negative* growth rates even in the face of an overall (manufacturing) increase in the total number of firms. This is, in fact, what the aggregate data do reveal with reference to the second historical phase considered above. What is crucial in the present context is that in the passage from the Golden Age to the subsequent phase the organization of manufacturing activities *generally* requires a number of business units larger than before; but it is important to stress that this is independent of the changes which over the very same period may affect the *sectoral* pattern of business activities (in the same way different countries may show different sectoral trends as to the rate of expansion of new activities, but all the same they may show a similar *overall* trend as to the stock of business units).

Bearing in mind these qualifications, we can now consider Table 4.4 (see also the synoptical view reported in the bottom line of the table). In general, sector data show behaviour consistent with aggregate figures: for all countries (again, with the exception of the United Kingdom), the number of industries characterized by positive values in the rate of growth of businesses is larger in the second phase (years following the watershed of the mid-1970s) than in the first one (the period of the late Golden Age).

It can be noted that this phenomenon is paralleled by some visible changes in the sectoral pattern of development of the observed countries. With the notable exception of Italy (but not for sectors 321 and 322), data show a general trend towards a fall in the stock of business units in industries ranging from codes 321 to 324 (and in relation to Germany, negative values of the rate of change extend up to code 332). Indeed, in all countries such a fall can be observed since the Golden Age. By contrast, industries included in codes from 381 to 385 show in most countries a tendency to expand the number of firms (as they actually also did in the Golden Age).

In the light of what has been argued above, this means that, at the same time as the overall number of industries characterized by an increase in the stock of firms becomes larger in the "Restructuring" phase, a gradual shift in the composition of manufacturing activities

Table 4.4 Percentage change in the number of firms in the course of the Golden Age (1st phase) and afterwards (2nd phase) (in italics: positive values)

Codes	France[a]		Germany		Italy		United Kingdom	United States	
	1st phase	2nd phase	1st phase	2nd phase	1st phase	2nd phase	2nd phase	1st phase	2nd phase
311/12/13/14	-13.8	62.4	-28.5	-17.3	-1.7	35.6	25.5	-33.0	-25.0
321	-38.4	-22.9	-55.7	-23.2	-0.9	-30.4	-25.5	-8.9	-13.7
322	-18.1	-29.3	-63.5	-14.0	-12.2	-50.4	2.1	-18.6	-1.5
323/24	-35.8	-43.8	-88.0	-24.6	-78.7	73.6	-47.7	-28.6	-30.2
331/32	-23.6	10.8	-53.8	-12.0	-16.0	38.3	4.1	-17.2	72.4
341/42	-4.0	24.6	2.3	40.3	31.3	99.1	64.2	5.1	56.5
353/54	-36.8	-22.6	-4.3	-9.0	96.4	62.3	0.0	0.0	-12.5
351/52	-15.1	5.9	-19.9	-13.4	-1.9	23.2	4.8	-15.8	10.4
355/56	26.1	50.4	66.9	24.7	303.2	15.0	b	47.2	75.4
361/62/69	9.4	-26.6	-14.6	-12.2	18.0	25.7	-6.2	-7.2	-2.3
371/72	-27.6	-29.3	-4.5	35.3	30.3	-16.4	-61.1	-4.2	2.2
381	96.2	38.0	-31.6	12.6	3.1	31.6	-13.7	13.0	17.3
382	-34.3	-16.2	-23.8	28.2	82.4	63.2	45.5	17.1	41.4
383	6.2	-12.4	89.4	64.8	33.3	91.6	80.5	16.9	53.1
385	30.9	118.9	-6.3	1.9	129.1	594.8	-12.5	36.3	107.9
3843	-59.6	18.6	-2.1	148.1	78.2	49.0	-31.9	10.9	53.7
3841/42/44/45/49	-19.2	-23.4	-15.5	8.2	55.4	142.6	36.9	16.7	26.7
39	-14.1	-38.7	43.5	18.5	19.3	-62.3	40.3	1.4	18.8
Share of positive values	28	39	22	56	67	78	59	56	67

[a] size class 1–9 excluded.
[b] sectors 355/56 are included in sectors 353/4.

Source: See Appendix A.

occurs, from "light" industries dealing with customers' final demand to industries mostly producing (intermediate) investment goods. In this connection, Italian industry (which is characterized by a peculiarly intense change in business size structure) shows a relatively anomalous behaviour, consisting in a fairly less pronounced firm stock shift *across industries*.

4.3.3   As we said, differences in the behaviour of establishments as opposed to firms – with reference both to their average size and number – will be more fully analysed in chapter 5. At this point, only a brief sketch will be drawn about the long-run changes occurring in the number of the former, in order to complete our general description. As we have seen for firms in Table 4.4, Table 4.5 shows the percentage changes in the number of plants over the two historical periods. The overall pattern appears much less clear than the one outlined above with respect to firms. At the manufacturing level, a trend towards a rising number of units in the passage from the first phase to the second one can only be observed in two out of five countries observed. At the sector level the basic absence of a general trend seems even more apparent: the share of industries showing an increase in the number of their plants (as it should be expected if plants' behaviour paralleled that of firms') is either almost the same in both phases, or even *falls* in the move from the former to the latter (namely in Japan and the United States). Overall, we can say that, after the Golden Age came to an end, no major trends towards a rise in the absolute stock of technical units seem to have occurred.

4.4   Average size and number of firms at the size-class level

4.4.1   In our analysis to date, the long-run dynamics of both the number and the average size of business units have been observed at the manufacturing level – or for individual sectors – without any reference being made as to their *size*. In this section the analysis will be extended to allow us to explore the phenomenon at the size-class level. The evidence which has been gathered about the different behaviour of "organizational" units (firms) as compared to "technical" units (plants) leads us to conclude that in such respects special attention has to be paid to the long-run behaviour of the former: first, as we have argued in chapter 2 (and as we will clarify more widely in chapter 5), the "rise and fall" of the small business sector in the second half of the twentieth century has much more to do, in point of theory, with issues affecting the

Table 4.5 Percentage change in the number of establishments in the course of the Golden Age (1st phase) and afterwards (2nd phase) (in italics: positive values)

Codes	Germany		Italy		Japan		United Kingdom	United States	
	1st phase	*2nd phase*	*1st phase*	*2nd phase*	*1st phase*	*2nd phase*	*2nd phase*	*1st phase*	*2nd phase*
311/12 + 313 + 314	−28.48	−18.47	−3.18	35.26	−15.20	−15.30	55.18	−29.09	−22.61
321	−54.89	−26.60	−1.76	−28.22	*50.22*	−54.10	−15.09	*1.27*	−14.84
322	−63.14	−20.08	−12.06	−48.54	*80.04*	*48.90*	*8.47*	−7.40	−7.03
323 + 324	−87.68	−28.61	−78.34	*75.91*	*65.76*	*2.09*	−35.73	−20.89	−35.74
331 + 332	−53.73	−12.88	−16.15	−21.40	*1.55*	−17.46	*23.58*	*40.30*	*26.97*
341 + 342	*1.41*	*38.51*	*31.58*	*101.90*	*78.87*	*26.56*	*108.28*	*28.54*	*29.18*
353 + 354/55/56	*63.96*	*22.10*	*290.96*	*20.54*	*192.55*	*328.27*	*62.58*	*86.97*	*23.12*
351 + 352	−18.78	−12.52	*2.40*	*24.10*	−2.37	*19.38*	*28.93*	*1.50*	−1.65
361 + 362 + 369	−17.28	−13.37	*18.80*	*29.89*	*30.35*	−6.70	*41.59*	*12.03*	−7.51
371 + 372	−4.08	*32.66*	*31.21*	−15.23	*79.38*	*10.18*	−89.33	*13.15*	−7.55
381	−31.05	*10.61*	*3.94*	*34.81*	*148.08*	−0.14	*2.91*	*28.05*	*2.91*
382 + 83	*10.29*	*36.06*	*63.10*	*74.47*	*136.86*	*49.35*	*417.29*	*41.55*	*17.90*
384	*5.16*	−3.31	*65.14*	*101.55*	*8.66*	*8.10*	*5.67*	*40.49*	*14.37*
385	−6.26	−0.79	*123.55*	*578.11*	*257.23*	*25.13*	*4.63*	*89.49*	*51.30*
39	*42.23*	*16.91*	*19.25*	*113.60*	*42.33*	−33.34	*520.96*	*17.23*	*0.57*
Share of positive values	33	40	67	73	87	60	80	80	47

Source: See Appendix A.

organization of business activities than with those affecting their *techni-cal* size; secondly, as we have just seen in this chapter, on empirical grounds – in contrast to we saw about firms – plants' behaviour shows no clear-cut trend following the overall pattern we set forth in the theoretical framework outlined in chapter 2 (see, in particular, section 2.6).

Hence, in the following pages we will provide a general analysis of how much, in two different phases of development of the industrial system of the observed countries, absolute employment levels (and, more specifically, the absolute size of the large and small business sectors) has been affected by any changes in the average size of *firms*, or by changes in their number.

4.4.2   As stated in the introduction to this chapter, if employment L at time t is expressed as

$$L_t = \frac{L_t}{N_t} . N_t,$$

where N is the total number of firms, then any changes in employment between time 0 and t may well be considered as the result of the interaction between changes in the average size of firms and in their total number.

In order to disentangle these two different effects (in analogy with usual shift and share analysis), putting $l = L/N$, total employment at time t can be written as:

$$L_t = l_t N_t = (l_0 + \Delta l)(N_0 + \Delta N), \qquad [4.1]$$

so that the variation of total employment between two periods may be written as:

$$L_t - L_0 = l_t N_t - l_0 N_0$$
$$L_t - L_0 = (l_0 + \Delta l)(N_0 + \Delta N) - l_0 N_0$$
$$L_t - L_0 = l_0 \Delta N + N_0 \Delta l + \Delta l \Delta N.$$

which, in terms of percentages, may be expressed as:

$$\frac{L_t - L_0}{L_0} = \frac{\Delta N}{N_0} + \frac{\Delta l}{l_0} + \frac{\Delta l}{l_0} \frac{\Delta N}{N_0} \qquad [4.2]$$

This means that employment percentage changes can be expressed as the sum of three different effects – the change in the total number of firms, the change in their average size and a residual term that reflects their combined action.

This way of characterizing the phenomenon provides a simple criterion for summarizing in quantitative terms some of the issues mentioned above: in particular, it helps us to obtain a measure of the relative importance which different ways of expanding industrial capacity assume at different phases of industrial development. More specifically, by measuring the contribution given by each of the different channels through which employment changes may take place, we are able to provide a stylized picture of the different models that, in single industrial countries, may prevail in the face of the two different macroeconomic contexts outlined in the first chapter of this book.

The possibility to break down data at the size-class level, on the other hand, offers the chance to explore the point in a more detailed manner, for it allows us to acquire separate figures for large and small businesses. In this way, it becomes possible to find out any trend any country may show as to the role played, in the context of our analysis, by size-specific forces.[15] This makes it possible to get a general view about the extent to which the general framework outlined above fits the whole set of countries here analysed, and to what extent any of them does show instead more peculiar features.

4.4.3 As a first step, we can find in Table 4.6, for five countries,[16] the decomposition of (percentage) changes in total firm employment into the two components they can be broken down in according to the above mentioned expression, namely the change in the number of firms themselves and the change in their average size (the third column of the table shows the value corresponding to the residual term of equation [4.2]). Because of the basic weakness of UK data, especially as it concerns the number of business units for earlier years (see again Figure 4.4), figures referring to the UK are provided for the second phase only.

The evidence provided in Table 4.6 can be summarized as follows: (i) all countries show a negative contribution of the "number effect" in the Golden Age phase, and a positive contribution in the following one; (ii) as far as the "size effect" is concerned, the pattern appears completely reversed – signs are systematically positive in the first phase, and negative in the second. This closely fits our general view about the whole phenomenon: in all countries manufacturing employment changes take place through quite different channels in the two different phases of industrial development we are dealing with.

But a more complete picture can be obtained by performing the same calculations as above at the size-class level. In this respect, by applying equation [4.2] we can analyse two further implications of our analysis. The first is that the "number effect" should hide a different behaviour of

Table 4.6   Percentage employment changes in manufacturing industry; effects due to average size and number of firms

Countries	Firm number		Average size		Residual		Total	
	1st phase	2nd phase	1st phase	2nd phase	1st phase	2nd phase	1st phase	2nd phase
France[a]	−11.89	8.33	25.48	−36.85	−3.03	−3.07	10.55	−31.59
Germany	−35.90	10.21	41.64	−8.63	−14.95	−0.88	−9.22	0.70
Italy	−6.66	12.12	28.59	−16.11	−1.91	−1.95	20.02	−5.94
United Kingdom	—	21.38	—	−51.81	—	−11.08	—	−41.51
United States	−3.27	30.34	21.00	−26.16	−0.69	−7.94	17.05	−3.76

[a] size class 1–9 excluded.

Source: See Appendix A.

small-sized units as opposed to large ones, in the sense that we are to expect that in both phases the observed fall in number of businesses mainly affects the lower tail of the size distribution (when firms get larger the stock of smallest units shrinks, when they turn to downsizing it rises; anyway we may retain the principle according to which firms coming into existence are normally *small*).[17] A second issue has to do with size, but this is far less clear in principle. Indeed, there is no particular reason to expect that either the "concentration" or the downsizing process (first and second phase, respectively) should affect either the largest (vertically and "laterally" integrated) units or the small, also owing to the relatively high threshold defining the upper bound of the latter. From this point of view, then, we have no more to do than looking at what data do actually show.

Following our previous analysis, these further calculations have been carried out with reference to the two main size classes we dealt with in chapter 3, corresponding to the two extremes of the size distribution (namely, firms with fewer than 100 employees and firms with more than 500). For both size bands, the results are gathered together in Table 4.7. As to the first (4.7a), it can easily be noted that in three of the four countries we are able to compare at the firm level large units' behaviour is consistent with this trend: with the exception of Germany, the stock of large firms over the 1960s increases. As to the second (4.7b), in all countries the overall stock of small businesses decreases in the course of the 1960s (most notably in France and Germany). A slightly less clear pattern can be found in data referring to the following period: in this case, the number of small businesses – consistent with our framework – rises in all countries again, but the number of the largest firms decreases only in three out of five (it increases in Germany and the United States). In this respect, however, it has to be pointed out that as shown in the last column of Table 4.6 – and as we have already seen in chapter 3 – absolute employment in the last phase results by and large stable in Germany, while it falls in the United States (but less heavily than in other countries). This means that, as is revealed by average size trend itself, the growth in the *number* of large businesses in these two countries by no means involves any tendency to rising concentration: in both cases, the average size of such very large units does actually *fall*.

When considering average size – the third and fourth columns in Table 4.7 – a more variegated pattern seems to emerge from the data. In particular, a curious pattern can be observed in the rate of growth of small firms in Italy. Whilst in the Golden Age the Italian economy

Table 4.7 Percentage employment changes in manufacturing industry; effects due to average size and number of firms, firms with more than 500 and fewer than 100 employees

Countries	Firm number		Average size		Residual		Total	
	1st phase	2nd phase	1st phase	2nd phase	1st phase	2nd phase	1st phase	2nd phase
> 500								
France	17.35	-31.41	0.81	-22.74	0.14	7.14	18.29	-47.01
Germany	-13.63	5.78	9.16	-5.66	-1.25	-0.33	-5.71	-0.20
Italy	23.94	-35.78	9.22	-21.51	2.21	7.70	35.36	-49.59
United Kingdom	—	-51.04	—	-4.32	—	2.21	—	-53.16
United States	3.49	10.42	24.64	-20.45	0.86	-2.13	29.00	-12.15
< 100								
France[a]	-15.30	15.45	11.77	-12.25	-1.80	-1.89	-5.33	1.31
Germany	-36.46	10.77	39.27	-8.62	-14.32	-0.93	-11.50	1.22
Italy	-6.95	12.51	19.96	13.74	-1.39	1.72	11.62	27.96
United Kingdom	—	28.61	—	-31.00	—	-8.87	—	-11.26
United States	-3.16	31.62	-0.43	-9.63	0.01	-3.05	-3.58	18.95

[a] size class 1–9 excluded.

Source: See Appendix A.

followed the same (growing) trend as in all other countries (with the exception of the United States, where the trend is basically stable),[18] in the second period Italy shows a remarkable divergence from other countries – that is, a persistent *increase* – of its average size trend. The lack of comparable data for Japan does not allow any direct comparison, in this connection, between the two latecomer countries as opposed to the group of more mature industrialized countries. Yet, Italian small firm behaviour suggests that – in contrast to what happens to large units over the same period, which behave in the same manner as large firms in all other countries – smaller units in a lagged industrialized country like Italy are (at least in some industries) *still* too small to undergo any significant contraction even in the face of the major shocks affecting the macroeconomic environment after the mid-1970s. This means that even in the face of an *overall* fall in average size in the manufacturing sector as a whole, and vis à vis a quite relevant increase in their very number, smaller units tend on average to expand their levels of employment (as we saw in chapter 3, Italy is actually the only country experiencing an increase in absolute employment in firms with fewer than 50 employees after the end of the Golden Age). But with regard to small business employment Italy shows a clear divergence with respect to other economies (positive instead of negative growth) even *before* the end of the Golden Age. In this case the reason has to be found simply in its very (relative) backwardness – earlier stages of the industrialization process being by their very nature characterized by the flourishing of new activities, largely developed within the boundaries of small-scale business units.

4.5 Summing up the empirical evidence: models of industrial development

This chapter has tried to set the analysis of industrial development in advanced industrial countries within the framework of structural change. In this respect, it has first examined the opportunity to distinguish between employment changes driven by variations in the average size of business units, and changes due to variations in their overall stock. Hinging on this basic difference, it has then gathered some evidence, at the level of individual countries, about the actual importance assumed by each of these different components of manufacturing growth in the course of the two major phases of industrial development described in the first chapter of this book. Finally, it has provided a measure of the relative importance of the different ways whereby industrial development has actually taken place in the observed countries. Overall, the results of this exploration can be summarized as follows:

(i) As far as firms are concerned, all countries show a trend towards rising average size in the course of the Golden Age, followed by a fall in subsequent years; this pattern is paralleled by a tendency for the overall stock of firms to decrease in the course of the first phase, and to increase in the second. In this connection, a (partial) exception is represented by the United Kingdom, which, however, is affected by heavy problems about the basic reliability of data referring to the stock of business units (both firms and establishments), especially with regard to the earlier years of the period under examination.

(ii) With regard to establishments, the overall pattern appears less clear; the average size of plants does not rise everywhere in the first phase under observation (this only takes place in Germany and Italy), nor does it show a clear tendency to fall in the second one (in fact, in the United States and Japan it hardly changes at all). On the other hand, long-run variations in the stock of establishments also show no discernible trend: only in two of the five observed countries do variations in the number of plants switch from negative to positive values when moving to the "Restructuring" phase (again, this happens in Germany and Italy).

(iii) In this context Italian manufacturing shows some peculiar features; in particular, it both raises small firms' employment levels in the Golden Age and their average size in the more recent phase. This is probably connected to the relatively recent development of the Italian economy, which had its actual industrial take-off after the Second World War. The lack of comparable data for Japan makes possible only a partial comparison with the other late-developing industrial country of the group (see, in particular, Figure 3.7 in chapter 3 about employment changes, which shows a remarkable analogy between the two countries).

(iv) Overall, the joint pattern of changes in average size and in the number of firms appear to be consistent with the framework we developed in chapters 1 and 2 in order to identify the logic of both manufacturing expansion in the course of the Golden Age and its restructuring in the course of the following phase; the same cannot be said with relation to *plants*. This can be explained by the fact that the macroeconomic changes we put at the very root of such a discontinuity mostly affect, by their very nature, the scale of *organizational* structures – whilst it is far less clear, in the light of those changes, which overall trend we should expect to observe in those *technical* units we identify with plants. In the following chapter we will make a more detailed analysis of this specific issue, in order to discern the nature of the impact of those macroeconomic shocks on the size pattern of manufacturing business units.

5

Firms versus Plants: a Closer Examination of their Different Behaviour in the Face of Structural Change

5.1 A conceptual framework

5.1.1 In principle, the division of labour may take place both *inside* the firm and among firms. In fact, this passage from one of these two different ways of organizing productive activity to the other is exactly the process that industrial countries have experienced in the course of the two different phases of post-war industrial development that we have dealt with in previous chapters. As we have argued in particular in chapter 2, this passage is precisely what economic theory should be able to explain: that is, why in different external contexts firms opt for different organizational structures.

In this chapter we will address a specific issue, which has been highlighted by our empirical analysis. This is the point that, in a theoretical perspective, producing does *not* exhaust the problem of organizing activities "inside the skin" of a firm: in fact, the existence of the complex *economic* units we call firms reveals by its very nature that competing in the market requires any producer to establish a whole series of functions *other* than production itself. We can find again in Austin Robinson a way in which to approach the question: following the view set forth in *The Structure of Competitive Industry* (1935), the size of the firm can be viewed as the result of an overall balance among differing "optima", each pertaining to a specific function. This means that the "rise and fall" of the size of *firms* – as has been dealt with in chapter 2 above – involves much *more* than the factors affecting their *production function*, since it also depends upon what determines the existence, within the boundaries of the firm, of *all* of its internal functions – be they directly tied to producing or not.

This point, one that is traditionally neglected by "standard" economic theory, which simply ignores the internal complexity of economic organizations (what Ms Penrose defined as 'the innovating, multiproduct, "flesh-and-blood" organizations that businessmen call firms'[1]), deserves some special attention, because the empirical analysis developed in chapters 3 and 4 has shown the existence of relevant *differences* in the behaviour of *firms* as compared to *establishments* (by and large coinciding with plants – that is, *technical* units). In order to clarify what the observed differences between firms and plants actually hinge upon, it seems worthwhile to consider the matter in more detail, in order to define more closely the role of the different internal functions of firms.

5.1.2   In conceptual terms, we can consider the expansion of a firm to be a process of *gradual increase in the complexity of its internal organization.* This stems from the principle according to which organizational difficulties increase exponentially as the scale of activities increases. In the famous words of Robinson (1935, p. 45), "the problem of commanding an army is not simply the sum of the problems of commanding the platoons in it". According to this view growth entails *in itself* an ever-rising complexity in the questions firms have to cope with. From an organizational standpoint, a major implication of this principle is that the "managerial endowments" of the firm are required to grow *more* than proportionately with respect to the total amount of the activities to be performed.

On empirical grounds, the evidence of such a principle can be found in the fact that, as scale expands, firms tend to gradually add to production a whole series of *further* internal functions (such as finance, marketing and human resource management). All such functions are basically characterized by an overall feature, which is the aim to maintain (and develop) organizational *control*. This happens simply because of the need for the firm to have at its disposal a constant "ability to answer" the (ever-increasingly complex) questions brought about by the simple expansion of its activities. This perspective allows us to see growth as a (discontinuous) series of events leading by their very nature to a series of *structural* changes in the internal *shape* of the firm: as the firm "chooses" to expand (to enter new businesses), a growing share of its resources will tend to concentrate in "coordinating" (i.e. in *non*-productive) activities.

According to this view, the key issue for an expanding firm lies in its capability to "keep together" its various parts in the face of the organizational shock implied by the need to cope with a wider range of activities than before. As we saw in chapter 2, following Haire (1959, pp. 274–5) it can be said that

> as the organization grows, its internal shape must change. Additional functions of coordination, control and communication must be provided and supported by the same kind of force that previously supported an organization without these things. (...) As the size of a firm increases, the skeletal structure (needed to support it against the forces tending to destroy it) grows faster than the size itself, and hence comes to consume a disproportionate amount of the productive capacity of the organization.

This issue is addressed in similar terms by Boulding (1958, p. 78): "growth in size changes the proportion of many significant quantities (...). In order to overcome these changes in proportions organizations develop specialized devices such as complex nervous systems".

Inasmuch as coordinating ("keeping things under control") is the central question to be faced as firms become larger, it appears that the degree of development of the "administrative" system is what marks the difference between large businesses and those (small) ones which can be considered as a simple technical (productive) unit – basically consisting of a single plant. That is to say that *large units are potentially affected by a far wider range of possible shocks than small ones* (for these mostly coincide with their *production* function).

5.1.3 Bearing in mind such a distinction, we can now face the question of the different long-run behaviour of the employment shares, the number and the average size of firms as compared to establishments. As we have seen in previous chapters, no *single* reason can be invoked to explain what has happened to both "technical" and "economical" units in the course of the two phases of industrial development hitherto analysed. This is because – as we have stressed – the size of technical units (plants) is essentially affected by technological factors, whereas the size of organizations (which generally include *more* than a single unit, and anyway far more than simply "technical" activities) depends on a wider range of economic forces.[2] According to the framework developed in chapters 1 and 2, we can state the question as follows:

(i) In the course of the Golden Age overall macroeconomic conditions push towards a larger average size of *firms*, involving in turn that a growing amount of resources (employment) tends to concentrate in large *economic* units. This reflects a broader scope for vertical integration, due to the existence of "planning economies" stemming from steady demand growth and a high "degree of predictability" of future costs and returns. In this phase, size expansion is paralleled by a constant increase in the resources devoted to *planning* (to "keeping under control") the firm's activities. It is important to stress, in this connection, that vertical integration is conceptually quite independent of what happens to the size of *single technical* units (plants, or establishments), which may even show an opposite tendency as against firms. In fact, this is exactly what happens to establishments in earlier industrialized countries during the Golden Age, as has been shown in chapters 3 and 4 (see section 5.2 below for a closer comparison).

(ii) In such a context, the size of each *technical* unit may rise only if what we have called economies of planning are associated to some extent with any sorts of increasing returns (economies of scale) at the *plant* level – *and* insofar as this is in turn compatible with firms' ability to cope with larger technical units on the basis of their "managerial" resources. Provided that no clear-cut relationship between planning economies and plant scale can easily be demonstrated on theoretical grounds,[3] we can say that in the outlined context plants' size may increase only if some *exogenous* technological *change* – meaning that *for some reasons* large-scale production is more convenient than it was *before* – is also at work over the same period.[4]

Indeed, from this point of view we know that as early as the 1940s – as has been already recalled in chapter 1 (see section 1.2.4) – empirical research had highlighted the existence of a whole series of technological reasons for the size of plants to *fall*, rather than increase over the long run.[5] And as it specifically refers to the Golden Age years, as has been shown by Prais (1981), in the UK case – in the face of a strong increase in the employment share of the one hundred largest *firms* over the years spanning from 1950 up to the late 1960s – the corresponding share for the hundred largest *plants* hardly increased at all. According to Prais himself, "this is an important conclusion. If we wish to understand why the concentration of firms has risen, it is clearly necessary to look to factors *other* than *plant*-size" (p. 46, emphasis added). That is, "in contrast to the popular view, ... we find that modern production technology offers little by way of explanation of increased concentration" (p. 59). (It could be argued in this respect that this body of evidence tends in itself to de-emphasize the actual relevance of the alleged "historical break" – pushing towards lower MES of plants – brought about by new microelectronics technologies in the early 1970s; see on this point section 5.1.4 below.)[6]

(iii) At the same time, a relatively low degree of competition from abroad raises much the same scope for integrating "lateral" activities (insofar as steady prices and exchange and interest rates set the basis for firms to reduce their overall exposure to market risk by *diversifying* their investments). In this connection, establishments' size, again, is largely independent of firms' strategies about their degree of conglomeration, which in themselves tend to affect the *number* of plants (of activities) owned by each firm, rather than the *size* of each of them. On the other hand, conglomeration involves a growing need to *coordinate* the (increasing) range of the activities the firm has to deal with, leading to an expansion of its administrative resources.

(iv) As we have seen in chapter 1, in the late 1960s *both* uncertainty *and* rising competition altered the macroeconomic environment, meaning that economic organizations are driven to look *at the same time* for higher flexibility and for higher efficiency. As to the former (provided organizational resources are limited[7]), the simplest answer is given by the process of vertical dis-integration: following Robinson once again, we can view lower organizational complexity as a means of getting quicker responses to external shocks. As much as fixed costs are converted into variable costs, the firm raises its capability to "decide quickly" (to face an "uncertain" world).

In this connection, however, it is important to clarify two more points. Firstly, this does *not* mean that the search for higher flexibility can be crystallized into a search for lower (fixed) *production* costs.[8] Even if it is extremely important, "productive" flexibility is but a part of the whole matter. In fact, the choice to reduce the range of the activities carried out within the firm is basically aimed at reducing the problem of *coordination*, for *this* is what enables the organization to adapt to a constantly (and rapidly) changing set of variables. In order to achieve such a goal firms have to outsource a share of their internal activities, for the smaller the firm, the lower the amount of resources required to coordinate them. This may take the form of both a reduction in the size of each plant (if many) or in their number: in any case, production is *not* the only activity which can be outsourced – in fact, we know that a large part of the activities which have been outsourced since the late 1970s has been "administrative".[9]

A second issue is that, indeed, vertical dis-integration *in itself* does not relate *at all* to the need to *reduce* costs, insofar as it is only a way for making firms more flexible from the point of view of their ability to respond quickly to external changes. This has clearly to do with saving *time*, but it does not necessarily involve the need to search for lower total *costs* (be they pertaining to production or not): *the point is just to change their composition, by making fixed costs less important.*[10]

(v) The problem of lowering costs comes from the fact that – as we have seen in chapter 2 – *at exactly the same time* as uncertainty increases, cost pressures due to rising competition also rise. This drives firms to concentrate on their core business, abandoning all the activities lying beyond the limits of *their own* competencies (that is, beyond their ability to *efficiently* carry out activities in the "new" competitive environment). In this case (large) firms' shrinkage would take place through a reduction in the number of the activities they carry out (which may coincide with plants), or through a fall in the individual size of them (which is the case when many activities are carried out within a single plant). In both cases, this means that "saving size" mainly represents for the firm an *organizational* question – first of all, raising efficiency asks for making narrower the boundaries of the terrain to be kept under control.

5.1.4 In summary: the Golden Age, pushing towards large-scale business both in terms of vertically integrated units and in terms of conglomerates, should have favoured a rise in the average size of large firms, a fall in their overall number, and a corresponding rise in their employment share. As it relates to technical units (establishments), and as far as vertical integration effects are concerned, this should be equally true (even if in a less pronounced fashion, for vertical dis-integration in establishments can only involve production stages, whereas in firms it may involve other functions as well). But as to the "conglomerate" effect, both average size and the number of plants (as well as the large-scale plant employment share itself) might indeed have been unaffected. Hence, we are to expect that during this phase changes relative to firms are wider than changes relative to establishments. When business units enter the "Restructuring" phase, it happens that they are driven by forces pushing towards vertical dis-integration to lower average size and to an increase in number, thereby experiencing an overall fall in their employment share. Again, plants' behaviour mirrors firms' behaviour quite closely (even if with less pronounced changes, for quite symmetrical reasons to those above recalled); but at the same time, as far as the conglomerate effect is concerned we might find no major changes at all in their size or number.

Therefore, over both periods firms' changes should show wider fluctuations than plants' changes. Were this the case, it would appear that – according to what Prais (1981) argues in relation to the UK case – factors other than technology have to be taken into account in order to explain the observed changes in the size distribution of firms. Or, to put it another way, that "organizational" (dis)economies play a greater role in affecting the organization of productive activity than technical ones. The overall pattern which the analysis hitherto developed should involve can be stylized in Figure 5.1, which illustrates the expected trends in the (output or employment) share of largest firms (straight line) and largest plants (dotted line) over the two periods above analysed. As the figure shows, the curve corresponding to firms is expected to be constantly higher than the one corresponding to plants (concentration is relatively higher in the former); secondly, the firms' curve is characterized by a steeper slope over both periods (firms show more remarkable changes with respect to plants); thirdly, it may in some cases happen that for both units the curve is lower at the end of the observed period than at the beginning (available data only allow us to observe the last years of the Golden Age, that is just a part of the "rise" phase); this might also involve a narrower distance between the two curves in the 1990s than occurred in the 1960s.

5.1.5   In this perspective, however, a further question has to be considered. Namely, the point raised by the economic literature (see section 5.1.3 above and chapter 1) about the role played by exogenous technical progress, up to the early 1970s, in altering the shape of the long-run average cost curve of business units – specifically, in lowering MES. Had such a force actually been at work (and its effects significant enough to make the average costs of new small plants actually *lower* than those of older larger ones), industrial structure would have shown relevant

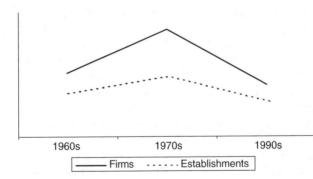

Figure 5.1   Expected behaviour of large units' employment shares over the long run

exogenous changes even in the number of the technical units belonging to a given industry. In fact, from this point of view – and under the assumption of a complete separability of cost functions – firms should have been pushed by purely technological considerations (that is, without any reference to "market" effects) to separate out their production process – previously carried out within a single plant – into a series of distinct units, each corresponding to a specific phase of the same process. This might or might not be paralleled by any breakdown of the firm as an organizational entity.

In this case, other things being equal, the result would be a higher number of (smaller) plants, the overall size of which – in terms of both overall employment endowments and output level – would correspond to the size of the previously integrated firm.[11] On the other hand, it should also happen – according to the current view of technical progress[12] – that (labour) productivity increases over time result stronger in productive activities than in administrative ones. Would we express firm size in terms of output, this might bring to overestimate the actual *changes* in the size of plants as against firms.[13]

These trends would per se involve, from the mid-1970s onwards, a rise in the overall number of establishments and a fall in their (absolute and relative) average size, offsetting, or even outweighing, the above described mechanism, therefore making way for a completely different pattern with respect to the one shown in Figure 5.1. Indeed, which of these two effects will prevail (in particular in the second phase at issue) is but an *empirical* question. The following section tries to provide some evidence about the matter.

5.2 Gathering empirical evidence

5.2.1 Drawing together empirical evidence about the specific issue raised above is in itself extremely difficult. The first problem stems from the very nature of the available information, which in principle makes it possible to compare data between firms and establishments for only four of the six countries hitherto analysed. Further problems arise from the basic unreliability of UK data as it concerns the information stored in business registers about the stock of both firms and establishments (especially for older years). As we have seen, whereas these deficiencies only partially affect the estimates we made in previous chapters about employment shares and the average size of business units, they do make it quite difficult to extract from data any reasonable evaluation about the changes occurring in the absolute number of firms.

Because of the problems affecting UK business data, the analysis developed in this chapter deals only with the other three countries for which we have figures referring both to firms and to plants – namely, Germany, Italy and the United States. Having to face such constraints, our empirical search for differences in the behaviour of economic units as opposed to technical ones will be somewhat restricted in its results; nevertheless, exploring the question in some detail – even within the boundaries of a very limited range of countries – may help us to focus on some quite interesting issues.

A first step in approaching the object of our analysis may consist in an empirical investigation of the relationship depicted in Figure 5.1; from this point of view, the point lies in detecting whether, in any one of the observed countries, the long-run behaviour of large units' employment shares actually follows the theoretical pattern hypothesized above. As reported in Figure 5.2, showing the changes occurring over the two periods here analysed in the (employment) share of both largest firms and largest plants (those with more than 500 employees), the available data provide only a partial answer to our question. The first thing to say is that, in fact, Italy's behaviour shows a remarkable consistency with the shape of the curves drawn in Figure 5.1; this means that in the youngest industrial economy considered in our group organizational (dis)economies actually play, in both periods, a more significant role than technical ones. On the other hand, with regard to the other two countries evidence appears less straightforward. From this point of view, however, it seems worthwhile to consider the issue a little further.

First of all, Figure 5.2 shows that, as far as the Golden Age is concerned,[14] US business behaviour is consistent with our model: a sharp divergence between the employment share trend of firms as opposed to plants does occur, owing to a rise in the former and a *decrease* in the latter.[15] In the following period firm share starts to fall, and plant share keeps on falling; the difference between the two trends – if any – can hardly be appreciated at all in the figure, but it appears that the change in the slope of the plant trend is also consistent with our general pattern (and with the actual behaviour of both German and Italian plants). As to German figures (which, as we observed in chapter 3, are characterized by a basic stability of employment shares), at first sight no evidence can be found of any differences in firms' trend as against establishments'. However, a closer inspection of data may help to highlight some more features behind the observed trend.

5.2.2   As we have seen in chapter 4, employment changes can be viewed as the outcome of the changes affecting the overall number of

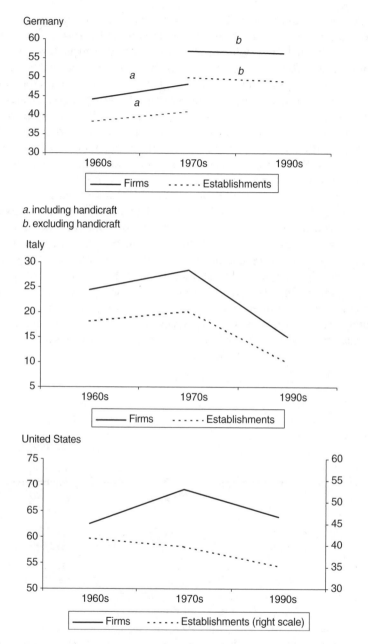

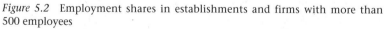

Figure 5.2 Employment shares in establishments and firms with more than 500 employees

Source: See Appendix A.

business units and their average size. We can develop our analysis first by comparing what happened to firms and plants as far as their *number* is concerned. From this point of view, we would first expect the overall number of firms (of any size) to undergo larger (downward) changes than the number of plants during the first phase under observation, because "administrative" economies – pushing towards larger organizational units – should overcome "technical" economies (which, indeed, may not even be at work at all). In the subsequent phase, for symmetrical reasons, (upward) changes in firms' number should outweigh plants' ones, unless they are offset by some exogenous forces acting on technical grounds, like those mentioned in the previous section.[16]

The outcome of the changes occurring in the stock of firms and plants (see chapter 4) can be viewed in Figure 5.3, which shows the ratio of plants to firms (that is, the average number of plants corresponding to any one organizational unit) at different points in time. Insofar as in smaller size classes firms and plants obviously broadly coincide, Figure 5.3 cuts away units below the threshold defined by 100 employees, focusing on figures which less probably correspond to single-plant entities.[17]

The recorded evidence seems quite consistent with the expected pattern, even in a country like Italy which, by virtue of its "latecomer" status in the industrialization process, is characterized by a peculiarly high

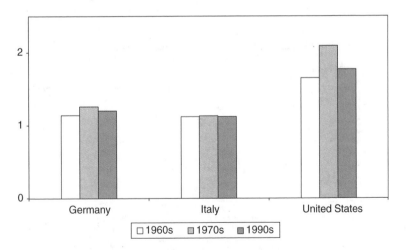

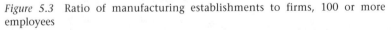

Figure 5.3   Ratio of manufacturing establishments to firms, 100 or more employees

Source: See Appendix A.

weight of medium-sized units (that is, by a strongly positive skewness of the size distribution, both for firms and plants, even beyond the threshold corresponding to 100 employees). Whilst it tends to minimize the difference in the ratios relative to Italy all over the period here considered, this does not blur the fact that changes in numbers of firms always outweigh changes in the number of establishments. The existence of something like an "organizational" factor seems actually to influence the different dynamics of firms and plants.

5.2.3 Given the observed trends in the number of the two different types of business units which statistical information allow us to analyse, we still have to explore the behaviour of their (relative) average size over the same period. From this point of view, our expectation is that – to the extent that the existence of "organizational" economies involves larger changes in the number of firms than in the number of plants (such changes being negative in the first phase and positive in the second one) – the very same factor has to involve symmetrical changes in average size. That is, it has to involve higher growth in average size of firms with respect to plants in the "Golden Age" phase, and the opposite in the "Restructuring" phase (when average size undergoes negative changes).

For in our view variations in size are expected to be wider in firms than in establishments, we can assume that $\Delta Sf = \Delta Se + OE$, where ΔSf is the variation in firm size over a given phase, ΔSe is the variation in establishment size, and OE is a factor which measures firm size changes which do not take place on "technical" grounds (that is, what we may term "organizational economies"). Hence, $\Delta Sf - \Delta Se = OE$ may be interpreted as a measure of the (dis)economies that can be observed at the *firm* level (which is the terrain we assume to be most sensitive to the macroeconomic changes described in chapter 1 above).

Figure 5.4 shows the values assumed by OE (changes in firm size less changes in plant size) in both periods;[18] as in Figure 5.3, changes refer to all units with more than 100 employees. In chapter 4 (see Tables 4.1 and 4.2) it has been shown that, when calculating average size for units with more than ten employees in the three countries under observation, both for firms and establishments an inverted-V pattern – with no exceptions – can be observed over time. That is, for all units, and in all countries, average size first rises, and then falls. In the light of such evidence (the same pattern a fortiori holds for the population beyond 100 employees), we can infer from Figure 5.4 that in all countries size changes are consistent with the expected behaviour of both firms and establishments, for OE shows positive variations in the first period

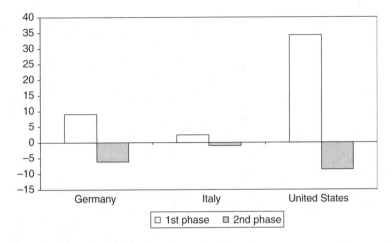

Figure 5.4 Percentage change in average size: differences between firms and establishments with 100 or more employees

Source: See Appendix A.

(firm size rises more substantially than plant size), and negative in the second one (firm size falls more than plant size).

Even more relevant, absolute OE values appear proportionate to the "age" of the observed countries in terms of their industrialization process. Even if this should be obviously tested against a larger number of cases, such evidence per se suggests that, when excluding the smallest-sized units from calculations, organizational "gains" (losses) due to being large-scale are as great as industrial systems get a given degree of "maturity" – which in turn broadly coincides with a higher average size of firms (see again Table 4.1).[19] In other words, we can say that to the extent that firms *become* complex organizations – that is, they add new functions, by growing, to the basic activity of producing – they have at the same time much more to lose from rising uncertainty and competition. In the course of expansion (enhanced, as it happens in the Golden Age, by "environmental stability"), organizational economies overcome the rising cost of endowing the firm with growing resources aimed at maintaining control; but as the economic environment undergoes a structural change, resulting in rising complexity and competition and therefore demanding more and more resources per unit of output to be devoted to administrative control, then organizational gains turn into losses, and firms are pushed to reduce the overall amount of resources invested in administrative functions at a faster rate than the resources invested in productive activities.

In what we may call the economics of structural change, "organizational" economies seem actually to play a quite visible role.

5.2.4 Some final words may be devoted to a consideration of to what extent the outlined pattern suffers from aggregation biases. As shown in Table 5.1, reporting the ratio of establishments to firms at the industry level, for both the (average) large business-sized countries (that is, the United States and Germany) the sectoral pattern follows closely the trend revealed by aggregate figures: in most industries, the ratio rises when moving from the early 1960s to the mid-1970s, and falls thereafter. This seems less true for Italy, where in only about a half of the industries considered here does the same pattern hold; it has nonetheless to be stressed, in this connection, that the divergence mostly regards the first phase under observation, while as far as the "Restructuring" phase is concerned, in most industries ratios fall (consistent with the expected pattern).

Again, the data clearly show the anomaly in the Italian industrialization model: falling ratios in the course of the Golden Age (as well as in the subsequent phase) can be observed in industries corresponding to codes 321 to 324 (textiles, apparel, leather and footwear), and from 353 to 356 (chemical and rubber industries). In both cases, it appears that the number of medium and large "technical" units reduces in comparison to the number of medium and large "organizational" ones; that is, that the organization of productive activities tends towards a lower degree of complexity. As we noticed in previous chapters, this closely reflects the increased importance of economies of specialization (rather than economies of multi-plant operations) since the very first years of the industrialization process.

With regard to the sectoral trends of the OE factor, Table 5.2 shows a substantial consistency of dis-aggregated data with those provided in Figure 5.3. In all countries individual industries are for the most part characterized by higher values in the first period than in the second one; again, these results (whilst they show no exceptions as to the United States) are slightly less true in the Italian case, where in several industries negative values can be observed even in the first phase under observation.

5.3 Conclusions

In this chapter we have argued that, in the light of the theoretical framework proposed in chapter 2, we are to expect that "the rise and fall of the Golden Age" involves *different* trends in the long-run dynamics of the

Table 5.1   Ratio of manufacturing establishments to firms, 100 or more employees

Codes	Germany			Italy			United States		
	1960s	1970s	1990s	1960s	1970s	1990s	1960s	1970s	1990s
311/12 + 313 + 314	1.09	1.17	1.13	1.11	1.16	1.20	1.71	1.93	2.07
321	1.13	1.16	1.15	1.23	1.14	1.02	1.68	1.96	2.10
322	1.13	1.13	1.11	1.03	1.13	0.98	1.35	1.66	1.55
323 + 324	1.07	1.08	1.19	1.03	0.98	0.89	1.44	1.58	1.71
331 + 332	1.04	1.19	1.08	0.95	1.00	0.27	1.28	1.61	1.53
341 + 342	1.08	1.27	1.21	1.05	1.11	1.16	1.76	2.11	1.92
353/4/5/6	1.14	1.32	1.20	1.21	1.14	1.01	1.95	2.66	1.71
351 + 352	1.21	1.34	1.27	1.24	1.28	1.20	2.39	3.22	2.17
361 + 362 + 369	1.15	1.44	1.14	1.05	1.12	1.04	1.89	2.14	1.72
371 + 372	1.20	1.19	1.19	1.26	1.35	1.18	2.01	2.49	1.89
381	1.07	1.33	1.15	1.01	1.01	0.91	1.48	2.18	1.49
382/383	1.22	1.77	1.25	1.12	1.14	1.11	1.78	2.42	1.75
384	1.31	1.10	1.40	1.19	1.29	1.40	1.97	2.41	2.09
385	1.09	1.10	1.11	1.19	1.10	1.12	1.67	2.65	1.86
39	1.05	1.06	1.13	0.98	0.95	4.97	1.23	1.55	1.29
3	1.14	1.26	1.20	1.12	1.13	1.12	1.65	2.09	1.77

Source: See Appendix A.

Table 5.2 Differences between the variation over time of the average size of firms and the average size of establishments, 100 and more employees

Codes	Germany		Italy		United States	
	1960s–70s	1970s–90s	1960s–70s	1970s–90s	1960s–70s	1970s–90s
311/12 + 313 + 314	25.7	−10.2	23.6	−26.5	39.1	18.2
321	−20.2	−3.4	−16.8	−32.9	30.3	−3.8
322	−4.6	6.5	21.2	−2.5	26.6	4.7
323 + 324	19.5	−5.0	−12.7	−27.1	74.7	−44.0
331 + 332	12.0	2.0	−15.9	43.5	30.5	11.4
341 + 342	13.4	3.9	49.8	28.2	54.8	20.3
353/4/5/6	−17.4	−3.1	−49.6	−20.9	98.4	−39.3
351 + 352	45.6	−5.0	3.4	0.7	40.7	3.0
361 + 362 + 369	11.0	−5.9	17.9	2.0	28.8	−1.5
371 + 372	−4.0	−28.7	5.8	−15.0	37.7	−23.5
381	14.4	4.4	8.0	6.1	33.5	1.4
382/383	1.7	−0.8	24.8	−19.0	23.1	−39.5
384	47.7	−21.4	−13.0	7.1	34.1	12.9
385	−15.6	−19.8	5.6	6.2	40.4	−20.7
39	−2.2	2.2	1.7	0.6	16.0	−11.9
3	9.1	−6.1	2.4	−1.0	34.3	−8.6

Source: See Appendix A.

size structure of *firms* as opposed to *establishments*. We have stressed that this is due to the basic difference in the internal functioning of the latter (broadly coinciding with simple production functions) with respect to the former (which include within their boundaries a set of more complex functions). Such a difference means that whereas the size of establishments (that is, technical units) by its very nature merely depends on production economies, the size of firms (that is, administrative units) is *also* affected by organizational economies.

Following our view, then, we have argued that the Golden Age, pushing towards large-scale business both in terms of vertically integrated units and in terms of conglomerates, should have favoured a rise in the average size of large firms, a fall in their overall number, and a corresponding rise in their share of overall employment. As it relates to technical units (establishments), this should be equally true as far as vertical integration effects are concerned; but as to "conglomerate" effects, average size, the number of plants and the large-plant employment share might be unaffected. Hence, we are to expect that during this phase changes relating to firms are greater than changes relating to establishments.

When large business units enter the "Restructuring" phase, they should be driven by forces pushing towards vertical dis-integration to lower average size and to an increase in the number of firms, therefore experiencing an overall fall in their employment share. Again, plants' behaviour should follow firms' behaviour closely; but at the same time, as far as the conglomerate effect is concerned we might find no major changes at all in their size or number. Therefore, according to our view over both periods firms' changes should show greater fluctuations than plants' changes.

The empirical evidence (unfortunately available for only three of the six countries analysed here) appears to be broadly consistent with this pattern. Changes in large firms' employment shares are generally greater for firms than for plants; the same can be said about the changes both in business stock and in average size. We can conclude from the analysis above that organizational economies play an autonomous role with respect to technical ones, and that they are much more strongly affected by the macroeconomic changes that occurred after the end of the Golden Age.

6
Concluding Remarks

6.1 This book has made an attempt to explain the long-run changes in the size pattern of business firms in terms of the important changes which have affected the international macroeconomic environment since the late 1960s. We have argued that relevant discontinuities in macroeconomic conditions have brought about a radical change in the perception of the external business context by people in charge of the administration of firms, leading to a re-shaping of the organization of production activities. In this connection the last quarter of the twentieth century saw the re-emergence of a way of organizing production and trade based on a high degree of division of labour *among* firms (rather than *within* them). This phenomenon reflects a major reversal with respect to what had only thirty years earlier appeared to be the only possible form of development of the industrial system: namely, the primacy of large-scale business organizations characterized by a high degree of both vertical and conglomerate integration.

The break with the past represented by this change was caused by several events that affected the economies of industrialized countries on both endogenous and exogenous grounds since the end of the 1960s. First, we must consider the demand shock resulting from the very mechanism of industrial development (which in itself caused consumption to move away from the typical goods of mass production) and the growing rigidity of labour (due both to the achievement of full employment – raising the intensity of labour conflicts within firms – and to the ever-growing standardization of work functions, which lowered labour flexibility). Among exogenous shocks some attention should be paid to the consequences of the introduction of new technologies in the production process, which are widely held to have contributed to lowering the minimum efficient size of plants. A relevant role has also to be ascribed to the asymmetric nature of oil shocks, which supposedly disadvantaged the more energy-intensive industries (mostly those characterized by a high average size of firms).

While acknowledging the undoubted relevance of such factors in determining an overall decline in the relative efficiency of large-scale production, however, this book argues that the full scope of structural change cannot be fully understood in its nature without taking into account the extraordinary "environmental" changes brought about – at the macroeconomic level – by two decisive forces, both basically endogenous in nature: (i) the relentless increase in competitive pressure induced by the process of international economic integration; and (ii) the increase of uncertainty on the financial markets following the crisis of the "Bretton Woods" system.

We sustain here (see chapter 1) that the industrial development pattern which reached its maturity at the end of the 1960s hinged upon two crucial pivots, which characterized what has been termed the Golden Age of industrial economies: on the one hand, the strong growth of domestic consumption of (mass) industrial goods; and on the other, the stability of exchange rates, interest rates and growth expectations brought about by an international financial system in which the scope for speculation was kept to a minimum.

The stability (and strength) of the growth process favoured by such exceptional macroeconomic conditions caused firms to look for a higher degree of stability of supply rather than fret about the demand side, ensuring at the same time a "reasonable predictability" of expected returns on large-scale investment plans. This translated into an overall tendency towards increasing concentration (both along vertical and horizontal lines), involving a constant increase in the average size of firms and in their output and employment shares.

That world was falling apart around the end of the 1960s under the weight of its own strength. On the one hand, the increase in competitive pressure brought about by the increasing business integration of industrialized economies (which is but a function of their degree of development) forced firms to concentrate on their core competencies – in most cases making use of a lower amount of resources, and especially labour. On the other, the crisis of the international financial system meant that the private sector had to assume the burden of the exchange rate risk and – due to increased inflation – emphasized the problem of interest rate fluctuations, thereby increasing the degree of market turbulence in structural terms and paving the way to speculation – eventually ushering in a phase of veritable uncertainty. This had devastating effects on investment activity, involving a fall in the predictability of expected returns and, therefore, an increased risk for large-scale investment projects. Fixed costs (increased by the greater rigidity of labour) rose substantially and the fear of capacity underutilization replaced the Golden Age fears of supply shortages.

While the competition shock acts so as to reduce the degree of conglomerate integration of firms, the "turbulence" shock contributes to narrow vertical integration (provided cost functions are separable). At the organizational level this corresponds to the transition from a 'managerial' economy (in which the low costs of monitoring markets are compatible with the "codified" system of response typical of the hierarchical organization of business) to a type of economy in which the entrepreneur (who can make an immediate response in the face of uncertain events) is once again at the very centre of the decision-making system.

6.2 Building on the work of Richardson (1960), Malmgren (1961) and Robinson (1935), in chapter 2 of this volume we tried to interpret the observed facts in terms of a theory of firm behaviour. Our framework can be summarized as follows:

By the early 1970s, increasing financial uncertainty (the "Bretton Woods crisis" effect), coupled with an upsurge in market uncertainty (due to growing difficulties in anticipating future changes in demand), led to an enormous increase in the range of relevant information for firms. According to the view suggested in the work of Richardson (1960) and Malmgren (1961), such changes force firms to devote more resources to information collection and processing. Insofar as this produces in turn a larger firm size (in terms of input endowments), the organizational complexity of the firm would rise accordingly. Following Robinson (1935), this would involve lower levels of efficiency. But as we saw previously (chapter 1), firms have to face one more constraint, which is a result of rising competition: this demands *lower* input endowments for any given unit of output. Therefore, in order to keep efficiency (at least) constant firms are forced to *externalize* some activities previously carried out inside their boundaries. This means that in order to face both challenges, firms are driven to *reduce the degree of complexity of their organizational structures* – in other words they have to *choose* which functions can be kept within their boundaries and those which have to be externalized (such a choice being bounded by their actual competencies). This leads to a lower average size of firms in terms of input, to falling input shares of larger organizations, and to a rise in the rate of formation of new firms.

We have argued that, from the point of view of the theory of the firm, this path reflects a model of firm behaviour we can broadly define as "Robinsonian", insofar as it hinges on the principle according to which the "optimal" organization of economic activities is a function of the *external* context. In this view, a crucial condition is represented by the difference between "stable" and "unstable" market environments (where "stable" denotes a low degree of uncertainty and competition, and "unstable" the opposite). Whereas in the first case the "economies of planning" overcome the advantages which may be drawn from "flexibility", in the second things work the other way round: that is, lower organizational complexity is the efficient answer to market instability. This means, in more general terms, that no one *single* optimal model of firms' behaviour can fit *all* market conditions – that is, *"optimizing" may mean the establishment of entirely different organizations in different macroeconomic contexts.*

6.3 An empirical investigation of the actual effects of the above mentioned macroeconomic changes on industrial structure has been developed in chapters 3 to 5. The results of this analysis, which has been carried out on the basis of an original data-set referring to six large industrial countries, can be summarized as follows:

(i) In the last quarter of the twentieth century industrialized countries witnessed a shift in manufacturing employment towards smaller business units. In chapter 3 we showed that this took place – albeit to differing extents – in almost all countries in *relative* terms, but it coincided with shifts in *absolute* numbers in only two of the six countries included in the analysis – namely, Italy and Japan, that is the two "latecomer" industrial economies. This overall tendency represents a sharp reversal of the trend experienced by *all* countries since (at least) the end of the Second World War, a period that had shown a constant growth of absolute employment levels in large firms (albeit far less evident as far as establishments are concerned).

In (relatively) older industrial countries, then, changes in the shape of the business size distribution were basically driven by the downsizing of large firms, *as compared to a relative stability* in the number of employees in smaller ones. Hence, we can say that in these countries the role of small firms with respect to *absolute* employment (which can be considered as a measure of industrial development itself) has been rather *passive*, their contribution having remained essentially *constant* over time. Such being the case, the observed shifts in overall employment mainly represent the outcome of the changing behaviour of *larger* units – that is, the reduction (at least in terms of the number of employees) of their average size.

(ii) Overall changes in employment can be attributed to two different effects: changes in the number of businesses, and changes in their (average) size. Empirical analysis developed in chapter 4 shows that as far as firms are concerned, all countries show a trend towards rising average size in the course of the Golden Age, followed by a fall in subsequent years; this pattern is paralleled by a tendency of the overall number of firms to decrease in the course of the first phase, and to increase in the second. In this connection a partial exception is represented by the United Kingdom, which is affected by considerable problems concerning the basic reliability of data referring to the number of business units (both firms and establishments), especially as far as it relates to earlier years. With regard to establishments, the overall pattern appears to be less clear: the average size of plants does not rise everywhere in the first phase under observation (this only takes place in Germany and Italy), nor does it show a clear tendency to fall in the second (in the cases of the United States and Japan it hardly changes at all). On the other hand, long-run variations in the stock of establishments do not show any remarkable trend: only in two of the five observed countries do variations in the number of plants switch to positive values in the passage to the "restructuring" phase (again, this happens in Germany and Italy). In this context, Italian manufacturing shows some peculiar features; in particular, it produces an increase in small firms' employment levels in the Golden Age and also in their average size in the more recent phase: this has probably to be connected to the basic backwardness of the industrialization process which did not take place in the country until after the Second World War. The lack of comparable data for Japan makes it only possible to conduct a partial comparison with the other "late-developing" industrial country of the group. Nevertheless, from the data we have we can discern a remarkable analogy between the two countries.

(iii) Overall, the joint pattern of changes in average size and in the number of firms appear to be consistent with the framework we developed in chapters 1 and 2 in order to explain the processes behind both the manufacturing expansion in the course of the Golden Age and its restructuring after the Golden Age came to an end; but with regard to plants things appear less clear. This is because the macroeconomic changes we put at the very root of such a discontinuity mostly affect, by their very nature, the scale of *organizational* structures – whilst it is far less clear, in the light of those changes, which overall trend we should expect to find out in those *technical* units we identify with plants. This is simply because the size of technical units (plants) is essentially affected by technological factors, whereas the size of organizations (which generally include *more* than a single unit, and involve more than simply "technical" activities) is determined by a wider range of economic forces. In the course of the Golden Age, the existence of "planning economies" stemming from steady demand growth and a high "degree of predictability" of future costs and returns ensures a broader scope for vertical integration, meaning that a growing amount of resources (employment) tends to concentrate in large *economic* units. In this phase size expansion is paralleled by a constant increase in the resources devoted to *planning* (to "keeping under control") the firm's activities. Yet vertical integration is conceptually quite independent of what happens to the size of *single technical* units (plants, or establishments), which may exhibit an opposite tendency to that observed in firms (and, in fact, this is exactly what happens to establishments in earlier industrialized countries during the Golden Age, as has been shown in chapters 3 and 4).

The same logic applies when macroeconomic conditions change: in this case the (new) search for higher flexibility does not merely boil down to the search for lower (fixed) *production* costs. "Productive" flexibility is only one, albeit extremely important part of the whole matter. In fact, the choice to restrict the range of activities to be kept inside the skin of the firm is intended to reduce the problem of *coordination*, for it is coordination that enables the organization to adapt to a constantly changing set of variables. In order to achieve such a goal firms have to outsource a share of their internal activities, because the smaller the firm, the lower the amount of resources required to coordinate them. But "saving size" is for the firm an essentially *organizational* question – first of all, raising efficiency requires it to reduce the boundaries of the terrain to be kept under control. Such being the case we would first expect the overall number of firms (of any size) to undergo larger (downward) changes than the number of plants during the first phase under observation, because "administrative" economies – pushing towards larger organizational units – should overcome "technical" economies (which may have no discernible effects). In the subsequent phase, for symmetrical reasons, (upward) changes in firms' number should outweigh plants' changes, unless they are counterbalanced by some exogenous forces acting on technical grounds. Moreover, we would expect the (relative) average size of firms and plants over the same period to involve symmetrical changes in average size – that is, higher growth in the average size of firms with respect to plants in the "Golden Age" phase, and the opposite in the "Restructuring" phase (when average size falls). From this point of view, the results of our empirical investigation are, on both grounds, quite consistent with the expected pattern.

The existence of something like an "organizational" factor seems to have actually influenced the different dynamics of firms and plants.

6.4 As we said in the introduction to this book, recent years have probably witnessed the end of the most intense phase of the "Restructuring" process which has led to the observed changes in size structure. This may even have involved in some industries and in some countries a reversal of the trends outlined above. But available evidence by no means helps us to infer any reasonable evaluation about future prospects. If the basic question to be answered, as we have argued in this book, is that of identifying the profile of the organization of business activities which at any one time is 'best suited' to the prevailing macroeconomic conditions – for no single "optimal" industrial structure can be considered as given once and for all – then understanding which sorts of "industrial model" should follow the downsizing process observed in the last stage of industrial development would require an investigation of what sorts of macroeconomic environment we will face in the future.

Certainly, what we presently know about current trends is not enough to start claiming that a "new pattern" of industrial development is emerging within the industrial system of developed countries. Furthermore, in respect of underdeveloped nations nobody can still say, for example, how relevant a role small businesses – rather than large vertically integrated enterprises – will play in the following decades in the emerging Asian economies (and, in particular, in China, where strong forces encouraging central macroeconomic regulation still appear to be at work). Nor does it seem to be easier to predict which kind of industrial structure will prevail when Sub-Saharan African countries eventually start their journey to economic development as we know it – if they ever do.[1]

But even under a more familiar sky, a lot of things still need to be settled if we want to ask the "right" questions. From this point of view, the first point to be made is that, on methodological grounds, a proper understanding of the problems at issue – especially as regards changes in the size pattern of firms – requires a clear definition of the *perspective* to consider them from: quite often, divergences in the evaluation of business trends simply reflect a basic confusion about the real issues that need to be considered. For example, are we interested in understanding the mechanisms governing the organizational logic of *manufacturing* activities? Or are we rather looking at identifying the trends characterizing the *financial* control of businesses (in which case we should more properly refer to some entities like business *groups* than to firms)?

Such questions point to the very roots of the problem of carefully choosing the unit itself we have to refer to in order to analyse size trends. And this highlights the need to consider the *economic* correspondence between different phenomena and different business entities. In this connection it can be observed that, certainly, neither the competitive pressure on firms nor financial and market uncertainty seem likely to die down in the foreseeable future. And such being the case, it has at least to be admitted that there is a possibility for industrial activities to tend *on average* towards further vertical and "lateral" dis-integration. But this might well happen, in principle, even in the face of a tendency for levels of *financial* concentration[2] to increase.

But there is an even more complex issue to be stressed in the above mentioned perspective, pertaining to the fact that business organizations – as their very trend towards breaking down shows – are made by different components, *sub specie* of different economic *functions*. This has to be intended – as suggested by Robinson's view – in a wider sense with respect to the simple fact that the function of *producing* can be made up of a series of (at least conceptually) distinct *phases*. In the light of our previous analysis, it rather means that both vertical and "lateral" dis-integration may take the form of the shedding out of entire *autonomous* parts of the firm. A specific role in this context may be played by the fact that each of these functions is characterized by its nature by a *specific* cost curve, so that cost curves generally differ when moving from, say, production to retailing, or possibly to finance.[3] In this sense, we can see the fragmentation of an individual organization as an answer to the impossibility of reconciling "differing optima", that is to the principle according to which "there is no reason to suppose that all the different functions of management and of manufacture will reach their optimum size at one and the same total output of the product. [So that] the problem ... arises of reconciling the different optimum sizes of the different parts of the same organization" (Robinson, 1935, pp. 107–8). In a world like this it may happen that the re-shaping of firms' boundaries induced by organizational dis-integration is bound to follow some *systematic* trend, reflecting the existence of *structural* differences in the cost curves relative to different functions. In the years to come, this might lead industrial development to take the form of a wide range of *different* size trends within the whole set of activities connected to producing – each corresponding to the internal functions of the (previously) "integrated" firm.

And, anyway, it is the very relevance of the category of firm as such which seems to be increasingly challenged by the constantly changing nature of the processes linking transforming activities (and related ones) to final demand. In this respect, the organizational changes which have characterized what we have termed the "Restructuring" phase have made it quite difficult to identify the particular role played by individual business units, whose boundaries have become increasingly blurred in the face of ever more variegated forms of inter-business relationships. This stems from the very nature of vertical and "lateral" dis-integration, which – by enhancing the economic role of market exchanges, whose efficiency cannot rely on merely occasional transactions – have raised the need for "stable" market relations, which may be manifested in a variety of cooperation agreements. From this point of view, the very nature of the "Restructuring" process has entailed a constant widening of the sorts of economic linkages among different units pointed out by G.B. Richardson in his seminal (1962) contribution,[4] leading to rising difficulties in identifying the "actual" shape and extent of *single* businesses in an increasingly wide number of industrial activities. This calls for considerable improvements to be introduced in the logic of collecting data about business activity, in order to widen our capability to analyse their "collective" behaviour on a quantitative terrain. As we point out in the Appendixes to this book, the current state of the art in available statistics suggests that in this regard much work is still to be done.

Appendix A: Building a New Data-Set on Industrial Structure: Six Industrial Countries from the Early 1960s to the Mid-1990s[1]

A.1 General issues

The need for international harmonization in the collection of statistics on industry structure has been emphasized by the United Nations since (at least) the early 1950s. After having published a large body of methodological studies on the subject (see, in particular, United Nations 1953), in 1960 the UN Statistics Commission published an international recommendation to promote a "world programme of basic industrial statistics (...) recognising the need for internationally comparable data on the structure and activities of industries (...), in order to deal with basic questions of economic and social development" (United Nations, 1960, pp. 1–2). To this end, it provided the member countries with some key criteria to be followed in the collection and presentation of industrial data (such as statistics to be compiled, definitions to be adopted, classification schemes of economic activity, collection frequency, and so on). This action was followed by a number of industrial censuses carried out by some (typically the most developed) member countries between 1960 and 1963.

Nonetheless, 40 years after the publication of this recommendation the degree of harmonization of such statistics across countries is still largely unsatisfactory, often hindering economic analysis in this field. Indeed, despite the UN recommendation and the encouraging censuses of the early 1960s, a high degree of heterogeneity still characterizes the compilation of the industrial surveys by national statistical offices. As the following pages will clarify, relevant differences exist in particular in the definitions of the basic statistics to be compiled and the classification of economic activities to be adopted.

Some attempts have been made in recent years to overcome these problems and to construct an integrated data-set at the international level. In particular, starting in 1992 a series of publications (*Enterprises in Europe*, here after *EE*) have been made available by Eurostat (together with the DG XXIII), providing basic industrial statistics for 19 countries. A second potential data source is the international database created by van Ark and Monnikhof (1996) for the OECD (from now on vA&M).

From the perspective of the present research project, both these international data sources must be considered as basically unsatisfactory. For our purposes (see in particular chapter 3), comparable data were required at the country level about the number of both establishments and firms and relative employment, broken down by size and industry and available for a period ranging from the early 1960s to the mid-1990s. As far as *EE* is concerned, the available information covers a time horizon which is clearly too short to be of use in the investigation of structural phenomena. Furthermore, the degree of harmonization guaranteed by this survey is far from being satisfactory: heterogeneity problems arise for the definitions of both enterprise[2] and employment.[3] Eurostat itself states that "the degree of harmonization of the national data-sets received by Eurostat is such that direct comparisons between countries can only be made in a very limited number of cases".[4]

As to vA&M, data are only provided for five industrialized countries (France, Germany, Japan, United Kingdom and United States), and the time horizon ranges from the *late* 1960s to the early 1990s, whereas information for the whole of the 1960s proves to be crucial for our present research. Moreover, this data-set contains information on the number (and relative employment[5]) of *either* firms *or* establishments. That is, different reference units are shown for different countries: data on establishments are presented for Japan and the United States, while data on enterprises are given for the European countries. As a consequence, a comparison is only possible *within* these two groups of countries, separately – so that no comparison can be made between the behaviour of firms and plants in any given country. Finally, several problematic issues emerge relative to the degree of harmonization. For example, the relevance (and consequent implications) of the heterogeneity characterizing the national definitions of "enterprise" and "establishment"[6] have been basically neglected by authors. A second problem is the imprecise definition of the economic activities that are actually included in the data-set. In this respect, the most relevant issue is the claimed attempt to exclude handicraft activities from the data. Looking indeed at the original data sources, this often proves to be unfeasible for some countries. A similar issue arises for repair services. Finally, as with the Eurostat source, the content of employment data is far from clear: in particular, it is not made explicit whether or not self-employment has been included. More generally, this data-set looks overly ambitious as far as the sector breakdown is concerned together with the attempt of presenting data on value-added (a flow variable) by size and economic activity. As a result, the authors often need to resort to estimated figures, thus reducing the reliability of the information given.

The lack of adequate information at the international level (especially for earlier years) has required the construction of a new data-set for both firms and establishments directly drawn from original national censuses, in the attempt to either overcome (at least) some of the major problems faced by existing data sources or at least clarify their extent.

A.2   The data-set

The new data-set covers six countries, namely those already selected by vA&M with the addition of Italy.[7] For every country, data on the number of firms and establishments as well as relative employment by size and industry are made available. The analysis focuses only on the manufacturing sector, whose branches are broken down according to the Isic (Rev. 2) classification with a three-digit detail. Like vA&M, three years have been selected for analysis, but the time horizon has been extended in both directions, ranging from the early 1960s to the last available year of the 1990s. As already emphasized, data have been derived from original national sources (see Table A.1 for a detailed description of the sources used in the construction of the database);[8] however, in two cases (for which both the relevant year and sources as well as the coverage coincide) data

Table A.1 Overall synopsis: reference units, classification of industrial activities and statistical sources in observed countries

	Countries					
	France	Germany	Italy	United Kingdom	Japan	United States
1960s						
Reference unit	1962 Firms	1962 Establishments and Firms	1961 Establishments and Firms	1963/1968 Establishments (1963) and Firms (1968)	1960 Establishments	1963 Establishments and Firms
Classification	Nomenclature des activités économiques	WZ 1961	Ateco 61	Establishments: SIC63; Firms: ISIC	SIC of Japan	US SIC 1957
Sources	INSEE, Recensement de l'industrie 1963, vol. 3	Stat. Bundesamt, Zensus im Produzierenden Gewerbe 1962	ISTAT Censimento generale industria e commercio	1963: Board of Trade, Report on the Census of Production 1963. 1968: Dept. of Trade and Industries, Report on the Census of Production	Statistics Bureau, Establishment Census 1960	Establishments: US Dept. of Commerce, Census of Manufactures 1963. Firms: Bureau of the Census, Enterprise Statistics 1963
1970s/1980s						
Reference unit	1977 Firms	1977 Establishments and Firm	1971/1981 Establishments and Firms	1977 Establishments and Firms	1975 Establishments	1972/1977/1982 Establishments (1977) and Firms (1972/1982)
Classification	ISIC, OECD Stan	SYPRO	Ateco 71; 81	SIC	SIC of Japan	Establishments: ISIC; Firms: US SIC
Sources	Van Ark and Monnikhof (1996)	Class 1–19 (Establishments and Firms): Stat. Bundesamt, Fachserie 4, Reihe 4.1.2 Stat. Bundesamt, Handwerkszahlung 1977. Classes 20 and above: (a) Establishments: Stat. Bundesamt, Fachserie 4, Reihe 4.1.2; (b) Firms: Stat. Bundesamt, Fachserie 4, Reihe 4.3.1, 4.3.2, 4.3.3.	ISTAT Censimento generale industria e commercio	Business Monitor, Report of the Census of Production, PA 1003 (Establishments) and PA 1002 (Firms)	Statistics Bureau, Establishment Census 1975	Establishments: Van Ark and Monnikhof 1996 (Census of Manufactures data); Firms: Bureau of the Census, Enterprise Statistics
1990s						
Reference unit	1994 Firms	1990 Establishments and Firms	1991/1996 Establishments and Firms	1993/1994 Establishments (1994) and Firms (1993)	1994 Establishments	1992 Establishments and Firms
Classification	N100	SYPRO	Ateco 91	SIC	SIC of Japan	US SIC
Sources	INSEE, Images économiques des entreprises 1995	Class 1–19 (Establishments and Firms): Stat. Bundesamt, Fachserie 4, Reihe 4.1.2. Classes 20 and more: (a) Establishments: Stat. Bundesamt, Fachserie 4, Reihe 4.1.2. (b) Firms: Stat. Bundesamt, Fachserie 4, Reihe 4.3.1, 4.3.2, 4.3.3.	ISTAT Censimento generale industria e commercio, Archivio statistico delle imprese attive (ASIA)	Business Monitor, Report of the Census of Production, PA 1003 (Establishments and Firms)	Statistics Bureau, Establishment Census 1994	Establishments: US Dept. of Commerce, Census of Manufactures 1992; Firms: Bureau of the Census, Enterprises Statistics

from VA&M have been directly used, although some adjustments and integrations have been introduced whenever the reliability of the original data looked uncertain.[9] One of the advantages of resorting to the original data sources was the possibility to obtain, in most cases, a higher degree of detail in the size distribution of smaller firms and establishments.

The general criterion followed in the construction of this data-set was the minimization of estimation. To this end, a lower degree of sector breakdown was preferred in order to enhance the reliability of data. This new data-set has generally improved the quality of the information with respect to the comparability both within and between countries; yet, some problems have still proved to be unsuperable, revealing the existence of persistent heterogeneities at the primary source level. It was not always possible to find, for instance, data on both firms and establishments for every country. As Table A.1 shows, data for both reference units were collected for four out of six countries: information on establishments was unavailable for France,[10] while the opposite was true for Japan, where reliable data are only available for establishments.[11]

A.3 Methodology

This section gives a brief overview of the principal problems faced in the construction of this new data-set, together with the proposed solutions.

A.3.1 Overall features

A.3.1.1 Definitions

In the construction of this data-set considerable attention has been paid to the analysis of the definitions supplied by national statistical offices for the variables under analysis namely, establishments, firms and employment. As Table A.2 shows, a high degree of heterogeneity can be found both within (that is, over time) and between countries. This is particularly true for the definition of enterprise, as the example of the United Kingdom clearly shows. By careful analysis it can be seen that the English concept of *enterprise* is not directly comparable with the term as understood in the other European countries[12] that have been selected. As a matter of fact, the English *enterprise* corresponds to a group of enterprises, whereas the notion of enterprise in European terms can be detected in the UK case under different (and indeed rather elusive) denominations, which also change from one year to the next: it can be found under the denomination of *establishment* in 1968 and 1977 and in that of *legal unit* in 1994. In 1963, the term establishment can instead broadly be equated with plant.[13] As far as employment is concerned, two of the selected countries (that is, France and the United States) only record the number of *employees*, thus excluding self-employment. As Table A.2 shows, this is not true for the definition used in Germany, Italy, Japan and the United Kingdom.

A.3.1.2 Industry classification

The International Standard Industrial Classification of All Activities (Isic) was developed by the United Nations in 1948 (and subsequently updated in 1958,

Table A.2 Definitions for reference units

	Establishment	Firm	Employment
France			
1962	"Etablissement" – Group of persons working in a specific place under the same authority. Industrial establishments of non-industrial firms are included, whereas non-industrial establishments of industrial firms are excluded. Registered Offices of multi-plant (industrial) firms are included even if they do not carry out any industrial activities; they are anyway classified within the same industry as the firm they belong to.	"Entreprise" – Legal unit possessing one or more establishments, in their turn considered as geographical units. Firms employing fewer than 20 persons, however, as well as those belonging to the industry "Batiment-Genie civil" are considered as single-plant firms even if they carry out their activity at different places.	"Salariés" – This definition includes apprentices, manual workers, clerks, salaried family workers, overseers, engineers, salaried managers. Home workers are excluded.
1977	See vA&M (1996).	See vA&M (1996).	See vA&M (1996).
1994	"Etablissement" – Geographically distinct unit, corresponding to a given address. Any given firm can not possess more than one *etablissement* at any given place. Two firms carrying out their activities at the same place do possess two distinct *etablissement*.	"Entreprise" – Incorporated productive economic unit, which may possess one or more establishments. It may be an autonomous unit as well as it may be the subsidiary of another firm.	
Germany			
1962	"Betrieb" – All plants locally linked producing goods according to the German list of Industrial Products, inclusive of administrative an auxiliary plants located in the same place.	"Unternehmen" – The smallest unit legally obliged to draw up book-keeping entries (balance-sheet and operating accounts) on an annual basis.	"Beschäftigte" – All persons working inside the firm.
1977	"Betrieb" – Every local unit carrying out its activity in the Extractive and Manufacturing industries, inclusive of administrative and repairing units located in the same place. Central administrative units are often registered as independent establishments in the same industry. Data refer to the whole of the establishment, including non-production lines.	"Unternehmen" – The smallest legally independent unit obliged to draw up – for commercial or fiscal purposes – book-keeping entries. Subsidiaries are considered as separate units. Both productive and non-productive lines do belong to the firm; the firm also includes other establishment located in the country. Foreign-located units are excluded.	"Beschäftigte" – All persons operating inside the unit at the end of the month, including owners, family members and apprentices, and excluding home workers.

	Local unit	Enterprise	Employment
1990	As above.	As above.	As above.
Italy 1961	"Unità locale" – Plant (or group of plants) located in a given place, where it is carried out the production or selling of goods or services.	"Impresa" – Economic/legal unit aimed at producing or selling goods or services.	"Addetti" – They include all people carrying out their activity inside the firm, both as dependent employees and as self-employed (entrepreneurs, co-operators, family members, managers, clerks, manual workers, apprentices and so on).
1971/1981	"Unità locale" – Plant (or group of plants), located in a given place, where it is carried out an economic activity.	"Impresa" – Economic/legal unit aimed at producing or selling goods or services. Such a unit may be a single-plant one (i.e. it may be constituted by a single local unit coinciding with the firm itself) or a multi-plant one (in which case one local unit coincides with the location of the firm as such whereas one or more local units are located in different places).	As above.
1991/1996	(1991) "Unità locale" – Place where it is carried out the production of goods or services. It includes administrative units, and also units devoted to other activities, provided they are located in the same place.	(1991) "Impresa" – Organization of an economic activity professionally carried out in order to produce goods.	As above. It is specified they include part-time workers and workers temporarily absent from the firm. Workers belonging to plants outside national boundaries are excluded.
United Kingdom 1963/1968	(1963) "Establishment" – The concept of establishment comprises in most cases the whole of the premises under the same ownership or management at a particular address; but firms were asked to exclude from all sections of their returns	(1968) "Establishment" – The smallest unit which can provide information normally required for an economic census, for example, employment, expenses, turnover, capital formation.	Average number employed – Number of persons on the payroll on the average during the year of return, whether full-time or part-time employees. Establishments

Table A.2 (Continued)

	Establishment	Firm	Employment
			particulars relating to any department not engaged in production for which they kept a separate set of accounts.		were also required to state the number of working proprietors, were appropriate, and these were included in the total employment figures. Outworkers are excluded.

	Establishment	Firm	Employment
1977	"Local units" – Factory or plant whose activities are carried on at a single address.	"Establishment" – As above. Sometimes activities which are conducted as a single business are carried on at a number of addresses. Where this is so, businesses are asked to provide the full range of separate information in respect of each address, whether or not the activities are different. Their activities may, however, be integrated to such an extent that they constitute a single establishment. In the latter case the establishment is defined to cover the combined activities at these addresses (local unit).	As above.
1993/1994	(1994) As above.	(1993) "Legal unit" – They are usually the tax units for VAT purposes, but where this is not so the tax units have been split or reconstituted to the individual legal units.	
Japan 1960	"Establishment" – It is defined as a single physical location where business is conducted or where goods or services are produced. Even a single physical location comprised of two or more units which are engaged in distinct and separate economic activities is treated as an establishment provided that those units belong to the same management.		"Persons engaged" – They include all persons who hold posts in an establishment, including proprietors, non-paid family workers, temporary or daily workers.

	Establishment	Company	All employees
1975	As above		As above
1994	As above		As above.
United States *1963*	"Establishment" – The basic economic operating unit which produces or distributes goods (...) at a single physical location. (...)The census of manufactures is conducted on an establishment basis. That is, a company operating establishments at more than one location is required to submit a report for each location; also, a company engaged in distinctly different lines of activity at one location is required to submit separate reports if the plant records permit such a separation and if the activities are substantial in size. In addition, each company was asked to identify and report separately as "central administrative offices" or "auxiliaries" those locations whose primary functions were to manage, administer, service, or support the activities of the other establishments of the company. Also, when more than one business was conducted at a single location under separate ownership, each business was ordinarily regarded as a separate establishment for census reporting purposes.	"Company" – Business organization consisting of one or more establishments under common ownership or control. Each company covered in the 1963 censuses was asked to report on all the domestic operating establishments it owned or controlled (such as factories, mines, stores, sales offices, etc.), as well as its separate administrative or auxiliary activities (such as central offices, central warehouses, research and development laboratories). All foreign activities of these companies, however, were excluded from census coverage. Each company was also asked to specify its legal form of organization (i.e., corporation, partnership, sole proprietorship, cooperative, etc.).	"All employees" – They comprise all full-time and part-time employees on the payrolls of operating manufacturing establishments who worked or received pay for any part of the pay period. Officers of corporations are included as employees; proprietors and partners of unincorporated firm, however, are excluded from the total.
1972/1977/ *1982*	(1977) "Establishment" – Business or industrial unit at a single physical location that produces goods or performs a service. When more than one business is conducted at a single location, each business under separate ownership is regarded as a separate establishment. Furthermore, if	(1972 and 1982) "Company" – A company is a business organization consisting of one or more domestic establishments that the reporting firm specified were under its ownership or control. If a company owned or controlled	As above.

Table A.2 (Continued)

	Establishment	Firm	Employment
	different kinds of business are conducted by a firm at a single location, each kind of business is treated as a separate establishment if separate records are available and if the size of the activities is significant.	other companies, all establishments of the subsidiaries were included as part of the owning or controlling company. In these Census the terms "Firm", "Company" and "Enterprises" are used as synonyms.	
1992	As above.	As above.	As above.

1968 and 1990) to promote and guarantee data comparability across countries. Nonetheless, each of the selected countries has chosen to keep its own national classification scheme and to convert this to the international one only when necessary. This constitutes an additional obstacle to the degree of harmonization of industry data at the international level for two main reasons. On the one hand, the conversion criteria provided by each national statistical office often appear ambiguous and are different from country to country. On the other, comparability problems exist even within the same country over time because of frequent changes in the way data are collected. In this respect, the new data-set was built in two following stages. The first objective has been to reach a high degree of homogeneity *within the same country* over time; in a second phase, the link with the international classification scheme has been introduced.

A.3.1.3 Coverage

As already pointed out, handicraft and repair services are often included in the original national data and are usually difficult to exclude (in the case of repair services, this problem mainly affects earlier years). Unlike vA&M, we have chosen to *include* these measures in our data-set in order to avoid arbitrary estimation procedures. Yet, even if this solution improves data reliability, some ambiguities still persist. This is mostly the case for handicraft, whose inclusion is made explicit only in three out of six countries (that is, France, Germany and Italy, where this activity has a significant economic – and sometimes even legal – role), whereas no clear information is given in other cases. In this respect, it seems reasonable to assume that it is included in figures.

A.3.2 Data estimation

In order to attain the highest possible degree of homogeneity, the data-set had to be organized according to a general classification, in terms of both sector breakdown and the definition of size bands. The first step in this direction was the "translation" of each national industrial classification in terms of the International Standard Industrial Classification (Isic) Rev. 2. In this framework, data have been broken down at the three-digit level. Furthermore, data have been distributed among five main size classes expressed in terms of the numbers of employees (1–9, 10–24, 25–99, 100–499, 500 and over). The problems encountered during such data reorganization relate to the specific criteria ruling each national classification system. In particular, "excessive" data aggregation (with respect to the adopted size and/or sector breakdown) and "hidden" data in specific sectors (for confidentiality reasons), have sometimes made it very difficult to organize the information according to the chosen classification principles (that is, to fill in all the predefined cells). Data estimation has allowed us to overcome the majority of such problems, with the estimation techniques that have been developed varying according to the level of information available in each case. Whenever possible, estimation has been followed by an iterative procedure of data cross-check.[14] The following sections describe the applied estimation methods in detail.

A.3.2.1   "Excessive" size aggregation

(a) Estimation at the sectoral level: A typical case of "excessive" aggregation in size occurs when the size classes adopted by national classifications are wider than those chosen for the general classification (e.g. France, firms 1994; UK, plants 1963). In those cases, the estimation has taken as a proxy the proportional dimension of the size classes among which data had to be redistributed. When this kind of approach did not yield satisfactory results, estimation has taken into account specific sector features as, for example, the "typical" size that characterizes certain manufacturing industries, the evolution of the sector with respect to previous and subsequent years, and so on. If the problem affected the last size class (that is, if the lower bound of the highest size class was less than 500), data have been mainly redistributed into the next size class below (100–499), on the assumption that the original size-class organization reflected a small number of firms with more than 500 employees in the sector. An extreme case of excessive aggregation has arisen with respect to German firm data in 1977, reporting as to certain sectors only information about the total number of firms and total employment. Since such a problem did not affect establishment data in 1977, the establishment size-class distribution has been taken as a proxy in order to disaggregate firm data.

(b) Estimation at the sub-sector level: The availability of a high sector breakdown has sometimes been useful in order to overcome a problem of "excessive" aggregation in size. In such cases, "hidden" values corresponding to a given sector have been rebuilt on the basis of sub-sectors. As far as the data reconstruction of two-digit sectors is concerned, three different situations have occurred:

(i)   "Correct" aggregation in size of the sub-sectors. When data referring to the sub-sectors did not show an "excessive" aggregation in size, it has been possible to rebuild the distribution of both number of firms (or plants) and employment of the main sector by simply adding up data referring to its sub-sectors. In such cases there has been no need to apply any estimation procedure; therefore, the result is not affected by arbitrariness.

(ii) "Excessive" aggregation in size of the sub-sectors. When data referring to some sub-sectors were affected by an "excessive" dimensional aggregation as well, the estimation procedures described above have been applied at a sub-sector level. Afterwards, the estimated values were added to the data of the sub-sectors that did not show problems of dimensional aggregation. Therefore, the resulting sector value is only partially affected by arbitrariness.

(iii) "Extreme" aggregation in size of the sub-sectors. A peculiar case is represented by German firm data for 1977. In some cases, within a given three-digit sector, the exact size class distribution of data was available only for one sub-sector, while for the others the information was limited to the total number of firms and total employment. In such cases, the size-class distribution of the main sub-sector has been taken as a proxy in order to disaggregate data referring to the others.

(c) Persisting problems: Estimation has not been applied if the problem of size aggregation involved not only some sectors, but also the entirety of the data referring to a given year. In such cases the original size breakdown has been kept (see Table A.3 for a detailed listing).

Table A.3 Persisting problems in size aggregation

Countries	Firms	Plants
Germany	*1962, 1977, 1990* *All sectors.* The smallest size class is 1–19 because of frequent data gaps at a higher detail.	*1962, 1977, 1990* *All sectors.* The smallest size class is 1–19 because of frequent data gaps at a higher detail.
Japan	Data not available.	*1960, 1975, 1994* *All sectors.* The highest size class is > 299.
United Kingdom	*1968* *All sectors.* The smallest size class is 1–24.	
United States	*1963* *All sectors.* The smallest size class is 1–19.	

A.3.2.2 "Excessive" sector aggregation

(a) Estimation: Data drawn from national classifications sometimes showed a very low level of sector breakdown, which would not allow a perfect correspondence to the three-digit Isic (Rev. 2) scheme. In such cases, there has been a need to disentangle single sub-sectors from an originally more aggregated (with respect to the Isic Rev. 2) industry. This kind of problem has arisen in respect of US employment data for plants in 1963 and 1992. The missing sub-sector data have been estimated according to the employment distribution observed in the three-digit sectors. In those cases where employment data of the main sector were missing, the estimation has been based on the distribution of the number of firms among classes.

(b) Persisting problems: "Excessive" sector aggregation problems have not been solved where the above mentioned estimation procedures could not be applied (see Table A.4 for a detailed listing).

A.3.2.3 "Hidden" data

With regard to German data (for both firms and establishments), employment values referring to selected sectors are sometimes obscured in the original sources, while the distribution of the number of firms is known. Usually, such problems involve only some size classes, and "hidden" data are nevertheless included in the totals. In cases such as this, a multi-stage estimation technique has been developed.

(a) General case: The general case occurs when employment data referring to the size classes contiguous to the one containing the "hidden" value are known. In such circumstances, theoretical central values (expressed in terms of employment) have been obtained for the size class that contained the "hidden" value,

Table A.4 Persisting problems in sector aggregation

Countries	Firms	Plants
France	*1962* Data referring to sector 314 ("Tobacco") are missing: for homogeneity reasons they have been omitted from calculations in 1977 and 1994 as well. *1962 and 1977 (vA&M)* The sub sector "Production of man made fibres" is included in sector 321 ("Textiles"), while the Isic Rev. 2 classification includes it within sector 351/2 ("Industrial, chemicals, others"). The same criterion has been followed for 1994 data.	Data not available.
Germany	*1962* Sectors 355 and 356 ("Rubber and plastic products") include asbestos manufacturing. Sector 385 ("Professional goods") includes watch repairing. Sectors 361, 362 and 369 ("Pottery and china", "Glass", "Non-metallic products") include data referring to the extractive industry, not included in the Isic Rev. 2 classification. Sector 381 ("Metal products") includes railways. Sector 382 ("Non-electrical machinery") includes "Office machinery". Sector 383 ("Electrical machinery") includes "Repairing". Sector 3843 ("Motor vehicles") includes "Pedal cycle manufacturing" and "Repairing". Sector 39 ("Other manufacturing") includes "Repairing". *1977 and 1990* As for 1962 (b)	As for firm data.

Japan

Data not available.

Sectors 21 and 22 of the Japanese (Sic 94) classification (respectively "Manufacture of petroleum and coal products" and "Manufacture of plastic products, except otherwise classified") results aggregated, whereas they are classified as two separate sectors according to Isic Rev. 2. An aggregation problem involves also sector 31 ("Manufacture of transportation equipment"), insofar a as it is not possible to separate from the whole industry the sub-sector 3843 ("Motor vehicles") according to Isic Rev. 2.

United Kingdom

1977
Sectors 355/6 ("Rubber products" and "Plastic products") are missing.

The subsector 492 ("Linoleum, plastic floor covering, leather cloth"), included in sector 355/6 ("Rubber products" and "Plastic products") according to Isic Rev. 2, has here been included within sector 39 ("Other manufacturing industries") in analogy to the Sic 1977 classification.
1994:
As for 1993 firm data.

1993
Sectors 353/4 ("Petroleum refineries" and "Petroleum & coal products") are missing. Sectors 382 and 383 (respectively "Mechanical engineering" and "Electrical engineering") have a slightly different composition with respect to the Isic Rev. 2 classification. Sector 382 includes the sub-sector "Industrial plant and steelwork" (usually included in sector 371/2, "Iron and steel" and "Non-ferrous metals"), and sector 383 includes the sub-sector "Small tools" (usually included in sector 381, "Metal goods not elsewhere specified"). Sectors 371/2 and 361/2/9 ("Pottery and china", "Glass", "Non-metallic

Table A.4 (Continued)

Countries	Firms	Plants
	products") include data referring to the extractive industry, not included in the Isic rev. 2 classification.	
United States	*1963* Size class 0–19 excludes self-employed, and the sector "Other vehicles" includes the sub-sector 3829 ("Missiles") of the Isic Rev. 2 classification. *1972* As for 1963. *1992* As for 1963. Moreover, sector 331 ("Wood products") includes the sub-sector 122 according to Isic Rev. 2.	

and for its contiguous size classes. Actual central values have then been obtained for the two contiguous size classes, dividing the actual employment data by the known number of firms contained in the corresponding cells. Following this, theoretical central values were compared with actual values, and the difference between the two has been taken as a measure of the estimation error. Finally, theoretical employment data have been obtained for the "hidden" value, multiplying the theoretical central value by the (known) number of firms of the corresponding cell. An average of the estimation errors obtained for the two contiguous values has then been considered in order to adjust the estimated data towards its "actual" value.

(b) Particular cases: It may happen that the problem of "hidden" values concerns two contiguous size classes. In such cases, the estimation error that has been applied in order to adjust the estimated data refers to the classes immediately preceding and immediately following the two classes at issue. When the problem involved the highest size class (for which it was not possible to obtain a central value), the estimated value has been obtained as a residual.

A.3.2.4 Estimation of French 1977 data about employment in firms with fewer than 10 employees

As stated earlier, French 1977 data are taken from vA&M (1996). However, after careful exploration data referring to the smallest units (those employing between one and ten people) have been substituted, due to their clear overestimation of employment levels – possibly due to the inclusion of some agricultural actitivities in some industries. In this respect, the estimation procedure has been as follows: first, the vA&M employment level in firms with more than ten employees has been accepted, and this figure has then been subtracted from the total employment level provided by OECD Labour Force Statistics. This number has then been distributed among the 1–10 cells corresponding to the various industries by allocating it in proportion to the industry employment shares observed in the size class 10–19, assuming that industry shares do not differ between the classes 1–10 and 10–19.

Appendix B: Measuring Firm Size

B.1 Some methodological issues

B.1.1 Measuring size is the basic problem affecting any work that aims to analyse economic phenomena where firm scale matters. Almost all empirical studies facing the question contain a discussion of the problems involved by choosing a given measure of size instead of another – inevitably arguing in favour of the one actually adopted. Indeed, whilst a few sources (basically those based upon a balance-sheet system of accounts) actually offer the possibility of deciding which economic variable to choose when measuring size, in most cases there is no choice at all to be made – quite often, empirical exploration simply models itself upon the available information. Be that as it may, in order to clarify the matter as clearly as possible, it can be useful to briefly illustrate the question on theoretical (logical) grounds, in order to provide an overall evaluation of the *economic* relationships amongst different potential size measures.

B.1.2 Generally speaking, a widely acknowledged view about the question at issue is that size measures are characterized by a high degree of cross-correlation. This fact is alleged to allow a certain degree of interchangeability among different measures, provided that they are consistent with the economic question to be analysed (this means, for example, that the relationship between size and returns may be more satisfactorily analysed by observing firms' assets than the number of their employees, since the rate of return is usually calculated with respect to assets; on the other hand, had we to explore the relationship between size and export performance, firm size would probably be expressed more appropriately in terms of overall sales). In this instance, high cross-correlation means that empirical analyses relating a given economic variable to different size measures should not show remarkable differences as to their results; or, in other words, that the economic phenomenon under observation shows the same pattern irrespective of the size measure adopted.

We can briefly consider the question as to what extent do different size measures relate to each other by showing the cross-correlation rates of various size measures relative to at least one of the countries analysed in this book: in this connection, we have gathered here some evidence taken from Italian figures; data refer to manufacturing, and are drawn from a panel of 8,411 firms with more than 20 employees selected by the Italian National Institute of Statistics (Istat) with reference to the period 1989–95. The variables included in calculations are the number of employees (L), the stock of gross physical assets (K), the amount of sales (S) and value-added (Y); Data refer to the first and the last year under observation. As shown in Table B.1, cross-correlation measured in terms of non-parametric coefficients (Spearman Indexes) is generally high; interestingly enough, the highest value – apart from the obviously high degree of correlation between the two output measures – can be observed in both years between value-added and the number of employees. This suggests that switching from

Table B.1   Non-parametric cross-correlation rates (Spearman Indexes) between various size measures

	Employment	Fixed assets	Sales	Value added
1989				
Employment	1	0.7155	0.7651	0.8638
Fixed assets	—	1	0.7893	0.8200
Sales	—	—	1	0.8904
Value added	—	—	—	1
1995				
Employment	1	0.7397	0.7962	0.8821
Fixed assets	—	1	0.8005	0.8327
Sales	—	—	1	0.9066
Value added	—	—	—	1

Source: Italian Institute of Statistics, *Economic Accounts in firms with more than 20 employees*.

employment to net output gives a bias in results that is lower than it would be for other measures; in our opinion this is important, for, as we argue below (section B.1.4), these are the variables which better express the "actual" size of a given business unit.

Yet, before approaching the very economic meaning of individual measures it can be useful to try and discuss the matter a little more widely from a theoretical point of view. Even if the question in itself falls broadly outside the boundaries of the analysis developed in this book, let us first define the conditions under which alternative measures may be interchanged – that is, results are independent of the measure used. In particular, following Smyth *et al.* (1975), it can be shown that "irrespective of whether alternative measures of firm size are perfectly correlated in their values or their logarithms the measures can only be interchanged under the restrictive condition that the measures are *proportional* to each other" (p. 7, emphasis added). In terms of production theory, this means that firms' differences in size may be viewed as different points along the same expansion path. In this perspective, in particular, the above mentioned study shows that different *input* measures (say capital and labour) may yield the same results only under the condition that the expansion path is a straight line through the origin. Even more specifically – even under such conditions – *output* measures will be proportional to input measures *only* if we assume the existence of constant returns to scale (in this case different sizes may be viewed as different points along a straight line on the production surface, corresponding to the same linear expansion path on the input plane as before).

B.1.3   Yet, this still means no more than that, on merely logical grounds, comparisons among empirical results obtained in different studies on the same subject – for instance, the analysis of the relationship between scale and returns, or the testing of some Gibrat-type relation between size and growth (to take just two issues explored almost daily in the literature) – would be, when size measures differ, *stricto sensu* impossible.[1] But it does not follow from this that *each single* study on the subject has to be considered to be meaningless: indeed, it simply means that, when choosing a given size measure, we implicitly *also* choose the perspective from which to consider the phenomenon we are interested in. That is, we have to be aware that had we opted for a different measure (where such was available) we would most probably have obtained different results. The point here is that the *actual* shape of the relationship among different measures in each specific "historical" context is a purely *empirical* question. That is, nobody can know a priori the nature of such relation (that is, how large is *in point of theory* the deviation from the conditions described above) in any given context. On this terrain, there is no theory at all to be invoked.

B.1.4   In this section we arrange a (short) list of the various possible economic variables which can be used as a measure of firm size. A broad distinction can be made among three main groups of variables: those referring to some measure of the inputs the firm makes use of (reflecting the scale of firm activity on the side of purchases); those referring to output (reflecting the scale of firm activity on the supply side); and those referring to firms' value (reflecting market valuation).

With regard to the first group, empirical research generally gets little further than referring to the number of employees or the amount of firm assets (in conceptual terms, labour and capital). From this point of view, the first thing that has to be said is that both of the above mentioned variables have little to do with the amount of the input flows – that is, with labour or capital services – actually used over a given period of time. In this respect, stock variables can be more properly intended as a measure of the "structural" economic weight of the firm – in a sense, they may be considered as a closer proxy for measuring the "supply potential" than output measures themselves (which, as we argue below, are more volatile in nature).

In this connection, however, a serious limit affects *capital* measures (fixed or overall assets). In fact, the book value of assets – as emerges from balance-sheet sources – represents the sum of a series of investments made at different points in time, each registered at historical costs, subject to occasional revaluation and different depreciation rates (owing to changing legislation) according to different time periods (not to say countries). This makes it quite difficult to get a measure of "actual" capital endowments of firms, for they will crucially depend upon the *time* of sequential investment decisions. Even more relevant, when considering total assets (that is, when including financial investments), a specific problem turns out in cross-time comparisons in case of inflation. This is due to the fact that financial assets – which incorporate inflation by definition – tend to grow more rapidly in time than fixed assets (registered at historical values), so that firms with relatively higher ratios of financial to total assets will be affected by an upward bias as to their growth. If, instead, the choice is made to exclude strictly financial assets, but to include inventories (both of raw or intermediate materials and finished products), another problem arises due to differing evaluations, among different firms and time periods, of inventories' book values. Overall, it can be said that a major limit of capital measures as opposed to labour ones lies in the fact that they cannot be expressed without a translation in *monetary* terms of their "physical" size. Such a translation, however, incorporates, by its very nature, relevant biases.

Different problems are encountered when approaching the size issue from the output side. In this case, a first problem lies in the very volatility of output measures as such, because they correspond to the output *flow* relative to a given time period. From this point of view, the basic weakness of output measures is that they are closely dependent on the firm's *market performance*, which may show considerable changes over time owing to at least two different reasons: the first one – which affects both production or sales measures – has to do with varying degrees in the rate of utilization of productive capacity among firms, due simply to changes in demand (or in the success of marketing strategies). The second relates to varying (changing) firm capacity in controlling pricing policies: in this specific connection, biases may affect value-added as well as sales, for output prices affect – given costs – the ratio of net to gross output. But the most relevant issue – which may assume a peculiarly high importance within the context of this book – has to do with *gross* output measures, and emerges in the face of *structurally* different degrees of vertical integration among firms (countries). From this point of view, the same size in terms of gross output might correspond both to a small firm producing nothing and exclusively assembling intermediate inputs coming from other firms, and to a large vertically-integrated enterprise. This means that, when we need to calculate a measure of the output capacity of a firm, it is by far preferable to refer to *net* output measures (value-added) than to sales.

A final (brief) remark can be made about measures based on firms' market value. Here, again, the most relevant problem comes from volatility, *sub specie* of the wide swings which may affect firm market value (which in turn, as recent events in the "new economy" sectors highlight, may show remarkable differences among industries and countries).

B.2 How size is measured in this book: advantages and limits of making use of (physical) labour endowments

B.2.1 In the analysis developed in this book size is expressed by the number of employees belonging to any single size class. This is not a choice: it simply reflects all we can do if we want to make an empirical assessment of the changes in size structure occurring in industrial countries, over a time span as long as the one we are considering here. In terms of what has been said in previous sections, this is the only perspective from which we can approach the question, if we want to make use of the available statistics.[2]

Such being the case, the validity of our results depends on the very significance of such a variable in measuring "actual" changes in size. Or, alternatively, on its being not "too divergent" – as to results – with respect to other size measures. Let us start, then, by considering the "positive" side of having at our disposal such a variable in the light of what has been observed in section B.1. It can be said from this point of view that the labour input offers three main advantages: first, it is a physical measure (that is, it does not depend on prices). Second, being an input (stock) measure it looks at the size of the firm in terms of its "structural capacity" of producing, regardless of how much it *actually* does produce at any given point in time. Third, it is independent of any problems relating to capital obsolescence, which would involve quite strong hypotheses about depreciation rates, especially when intertemporal comparisons are to be made. It can be added that labour endowments provide clearly intelligible information as to the role any given firm (or size class, or whatever) plays in contributing to overall employment – which, in the face of an overall de-industrialization trend all over the developed world, seems to be quite an important point.

On the other hand, it is often said that labour measures of firm size may entail major shortcomings due to possible differences amongst firms in productivity growth trends: from this point of view it is generally argued, first, that a fall in (absolute) employment levels may nevertheless result in – because of (labour) productivity increases – unchanged output levels, so that the shape of the phenomenon crucially depends on the variable adopted; secondly, it is suggested that small firms are presumably characterized by lower productivity growth than larger ones, so that making comparisons over time at the size-class level on the basis of simple employment trends may lead to an overestimation of the extent of large firms' downsizing. This means that (large) firms may appear to be saving size when in fact they are simply saving *labour* – in which case downsizing merely reflects a shift along isoquants, *within* the same production function (surface) as before.

B.2.2 In the light of the caveats expressed above, some questions need to be defined both on logical and empirical grounds. With regard to the theory, it has to be recalled here that the analysis developed in this book refers to the *shift* of important *shares* of industrial activity from large-scale enterprises to small businesses, which has been brought about by some specific changes in global macroeconomic conditions. Such a shift may have taken place, in different periods and countries, in the face of either *total* output (as well as employment) stagnation, or growth, or both.[3] What really matters, from our point of view, is simply the (possible) existence of cross-size *differences* in output trends, for *this* would mean that, *when viewed from (at least) another point of view*, the firm size pattern might show a different trend over time – whereas no major implications would arise for our analysis if output (productivity) trends simply followed a similar behaviour *across* the size range.

In order to get some evaluation of the differences in results we might observe when measuring the relative "economic weight" of firms according to different measures of their size (in this case, employment and output), we show in this section some evidence taken, again, from the Italian firms' Economic Accounts (EA) series. In this case, our calculations are based on a reconstruction – provided by the Italian National Institute of Statistics – of harmonized data over a period (between 1975 and 1988) which can be considered as the "core" of the "Restructuring" phase following the Golden Age.[4] A major issue that needs to be stressed in this connection is that the correct output measure to be chosen here is value-added, for gross output measures (production or sales, also available from the EA series) would involve serious biases of actual output trends over time. This is due to the fact that vertical dis-integration (which plays a key role in structural change and is particularly relevant in the Italian case) leads to a structural rise of overall sales for any given level of net output, insofar as it brings about a larger amount of market exchanges.

The first question to be answered is how large is the difference between the changes in the size pattern we have observed in chapters 3 and 4 and the changes we might observe when measuring size in terms of value added. For we can express L_0 as $(L_0/Y_0)Y_0$, (where L is the number of employees of a given firm, and Y its output level), and L_n as $(L_n/Y_n)Y_n$, we can get a measure of the difference at issue by simply computing the theoretical value in n of employment under the hypothesis of no variation in labour productivity (that is, $L_0/Y_0 = L_n/Y_n$). This theoretical value of L can be written as:

$$\hat{L}_n = L_0\,(Y_n/Y_0).$$

Drawing data from the EA data-set, and referring to the years 1975 to 1988, Table B.2 provides an overall picture of the changes occurring in employment shares at the size-class level under such assumptions, other than a measure of actual shares in the first and last year under examination, and of observed changes in absolute employment, value-added and labour productivity. Results show that almost no differences turn out between actual and theoretical shares relative to both smaller and larger firms at the end of the period (second and third columns in the table, respectively): if any, the difference is actually *opposite* to what usual presumptions about the question would predict. In fact, the employment share of smaller firms at the end of the period (36.2 per cent as against 25.2 per cent in the initial year) would have become slightly *larger* (36.5 per cent) had no changes in productivity occurred.

This involves that – in Italy and from the mid-1970s to the late 1980s – the alleged "productivity bias" looks negligible; and in point of fact the same table shows that such changes in employment shares correspond to a strong difference in output growth between the two extreme size bands (medium-sized firms seem to show no discernible difference as to their changes whatever the point of view from which we consider their behaviour). While at the same time labour productivity shows an almost identical rhythm of change in all classes, over the period we are examining smaller firms do increase *both* their employment and their output, whereas the quite small positive variation of real output in large ones entails an overall *fall* in absolute employment. On the whole, these data highlight the point that larger firms' contribution to manufacturing activity shrinks even when measured in terms of output.

Table B.2 Employment shares (L), and indexes of absolute employment (dL), real output (dY) and labour productivity (dπ) in Italian manufacturing per size classes, "Restructuring" phase (1975–88)

Size classes	L (1975)	L (1988)	L* (1988)[a]	dL[b]	dY[b]	dπ[b]
20–99	25.2	36.2	36.5	114	237	208
100–499	27.1	29.7	29.8	86	179	207
>499	47.7	34.1	33.7	56	115	205

[a] Theoretical shares in 1988 corresponding to the hypothesis of no variations in output levels between 1975 and 1988.
[b] 1975 = 100.
Source: Italian Institute of Statistics (various years), *Economic Accounts in firms with more than 20 employees.*

B.2.3 Our calculations show that in those years corresponding to the "Restructuring" phase, albeit (slightly) growing in absolute terms, large firms' output does not keep pace with *total* output growth (which is driven by small business activity); that is, their size in terms of output gets lower than it would have been had it grown proportionately to the output of the entire economy.

This is a key point, which helps us to clarify a further question lying behind the measurement issue. This question has to do with the fact that changes in output size must be evaluated in the light of overall *market* growth in terms of output. That is, what matters in our view is how large output size gets as compared to the *potential* size the firm would attain if its relative size with respect to the market (that is, concentration) remained unchanged. This qualification is important for, according to the view set forth in this book, changes in size structure depend upon changes in the organization of manufacturing activities: this is to say that were manufacturing organizations the same throughout the period analysed here, we should expect size to have *risen* simply due to the widening of market boundaries – a process which, as we saw, is very much enhanced by international economic integration. In other words, it may well happen that output size rises even in the course of what we have termed the "Restructuring" phase (during which time we know the average size in terms of the number of employees generally *falls*); but this would still mean nothing in terms of actual trends in size, for – given market growth – even in this case overall concentration might have *fallen* anyway. This stems from the very nature of the restructuring process, which, as shown in chapter 1 (see in particular section 1.3), requires a higher *number* of business units to produce for any given amount of output transformation to be made. In this connection it is very interesting to recall a contribution which drew the attention on the question far before the restructuring process did start, by noting that "it is not clearly true that each increment of growth in the national economy tends to increase the average size of enterprises ... By sub-division of processes, more narrow specialization of establishments and separate ownership of the specialized activities also become possible" (Edwards, 1963, pp. 121–2).

Appendix C: Cross-References between Isic (Rev. 2) Codes and Industrial Activities

Table C.1 Codes and activities (Isic Rev. 2)

Codes	Activities
311/12	Food
313	Beverages
314	Tobacco
321	Textiles
322	Clothing
323	Leather and products
324	Footwear
331	Wood products
341	Paper products
342	Printing and publishing
353	Petroleum refineries
354	Petroleum and coal products
351	Industrial chemicals
352	Other chemicals
3522	Drugs and medicines
355	Rubber products
356	Plastic products, n.e.c.
361	Pottery and china
362	Glass and products
369	Non-metallic products, n.e.c.
371	Iron and steel
372	Non-ferrous metals
381	Metal products
382	Non-electrical machinery
3825	Office and computing equipment
383	Electrical machinery
3832	Radio, TV and communication equipment
385	Professional goods
3843	Motor vehicles
3841	Shipbuilding and repairing
3842	Railroad equipment
3844	Motorcycles and bicycles

Table C.1   (Continued)

Codes	Activities
3845	Aircraft
3849	Transport equipment, n.e.c.
332	Furniture and fixtures
39	Other manufacturing
3	Total manufacturing

In the calculation of Adelman's Index the following industries of the Isic classification (Rev. 2) were excluded for all of the countries considered: 314 (Tobacco), 353 (Petroleum refineries), 354 (Petroleum and coal products), 371 (Iron and steel) and 372 (Non-ferrous metals).

In the case of France codes 361 and 369 also had to be excluded because in 1973 data relative to 369 include, in addition to those relative to 361, also those concerning 29 (Other mining). The analysis excluded 1968 because of the difficulty of comparing the classification of activities used in 1968 with that used in the following years (in 1968 the data of code 39 were added to those of industries 355 and 356, and later code 39 was included in 331 + 332). It was not possible to exclude code 314 because the original data were aggregated with codes 311, 312 and 313.

In the case of Germany, it was possible to calculate Adelman's Index only for 1977 and 1990, because in the original sources the data concerning production refer only to firms with more than 20 employees, while the data on value added refer to all factories. In order to standardize both the numerator and the denominator the production values of size classes contained in the work by van Ark and Monnikhof (1996) have been used. Industries 314, 342, 351 and 352 have had to be excluded because no data were available for the industries' totals concerning 1990 production in the sources used.

Table C.2 Isic (Rev. 2) Codes referring to activities included in the calculation of Adelman Index in Figure 1.6

Italy[1]	Japan[2]	France[3]	United Kingdom[4]	United States[5]	Germany[6]
311 + 312	311 + 312	311 + 312 + 313 + 314	311 + 312	311 + 312	311 + 312
313	313	321 + 322	313	313	313
321	321	323 + 324	321	321	321
322	322	331 + 332 + 390	322	322	322
323 + 324	323 + 324	341	323 + 324	323	323 + 324
331 + 332	331 + 332	342	331 + 332	324	331 + 332
341	341	351	341	331	355
342	342	352	342	332	356
351 + 352	351 + 352	355 + 356	351 + 352	341	361
355 + 356	355 + 356	362	355 + 356	342	362
361 + 362 + 369	361 + 362 + 369	381	361	351 + 352	369
381 + 382	381 + 382	382 + 385	362 + 369	355	381
383	383	383	381 + 382	356	382
384	384	384	383	361	383
385	385 + 390		384	362	384
390			385	369	385
			390	381	390
				382	
				383	
				384	
				385	
				390	

[1] Value Added and Gross Output at factor costs, firms with more than 20 employees.
[2] Value Added at factor costs, Gross Output at market prices; 1983 and 1991 establishments with more than 4 employees.
[3] Value Added and Gross Output at factor costs.
[4] Value Added and Gross Output at factor costs; 1994 establishments with more than 20 employees.
[5] Value Added and Gross Output at factor costs.
[6] Value Added and Gross Output at factor costs.

Notes

Acknowledgements

1 See, in particular, Traù (1999, 2000, 2001).

Introduction

1 It is impossible to give a complete account here of the contributions on the matter. A very stylized picture of the state of the art at the end of the century may include: (i) empirical analyses developed within some international institutions (namely, OECD and ILO) in order to provide an adequately sound evidence for the phenomenon (especially in the light of an international comparison of its actual intensity): from this point of view, we can recall here (below, chapter 3) the works by OECD (1985) and Sengenberger *et al.* (1990); (ii) books such as those by Piore and Sabel (1984), and Best (1990), which represent an attempt to set the alleged changes within the framework of a "new paradigm" of industrial development; (iii) the birth of several scientific journals aimed at analysing the present state and the future of the small business sector in the industrial system (above all in this connection, *Small Business Economics*, directed by two leading scholars in the field, Z. Acs and D. Audretsch, who are also authors or editors of several books on the subject).

2 Examples of these sorts of analyses can be found in Sengenberger *et al.* (1990), Acs and Audretsch (1990).

3 The basic reference for approaching the Golden Age issue still remains the essay by Glyn *et al.* (1990).

4 Both factors are recalled in a contribution by Carlsson (1996, see more widely chapter 1 here), but without any reference to the Golden Age issue (on the other hand, no explicit reference to them is made in the above mentioned contribution by Glyn *et al.*). In a similar perspective, the question of uncertainty is also raised by Vercelli (1988).

5 On this point see, for instance, Schrader (1993).

6 See on the point a very recent paper by Kay (2001).

1 The Macroeconomic Context in Historical Perspective: Exogenous and Endogenous Changes in Firms' 'Competitive Environment'

1 As recently as the late 1970s, the empirical investigation carried out by Prais (1981) still led the author to conclude that "in the current ... period [i.e. in the years following 1950] it appears that factors systematically favouring a relatively faster rate of growth by large firms have become dominant; these have combined with the general diffusion process to make for an unprecedented rate of increase in concentration, to which no limit can be seen at present" (p. 40).

2 In this connection a number of extremely interesting critical considerations were made by Meade (1968) in a review of Galbraith's 1967 book; owing to their exceptional relevance with respect to our analysis, we quote from that contribution below, in a more appropriate context (see section 1.2.5).

3 No attempt will be made here to review the literature on the subject; we will simply note the title of the volume edited in 1971 by Marris and Wood (*The Corporate Economy*), which tried to set forth a first assessment of the issue, including papers by some important theoretical scholars of the time. See anyway below (chapter 2).

4 It could be said that the bulk of organizational research acts as a catalyst drawing attention to the "problem" of large firms, thus favouring the recovery of the conceptual assumptions made by Berle and Means as early as the beginning of the 1930s. The obvious (basic) references to be made here are to Simon (1945) and Cyert and March (1963). For a more detailed analysis of the whole matter see chapter 2 below.

5 See Momigliano (1971, p. x, my own translation).

6 See again Momigliano (1971, p. viii, my own translation; emphasis added).

7 According to Engel's Law, this means a high degree of income elasticity of demand for manufactured goods. In particular, this phenomenon is enhanced by the specific relevance, *within* the manufacturing sector, assumed by the production of basic inputs and mass standardized goods – often associated with large firm size.

8 See specifically on this point the perspective opened by Richardson's analysis (1960), here analysed in chapter 2.

9 Actually, the need to stabilize upstream and downstream markets begins to appear as an organizational problem long before the second post-war period. As is argued by Kocka (1978) about German industry in the early years of the century, 'even the slightest upset in production meant massive losses; diversification into raw materials and transport allowed this risk to be minimized; diversification of this sort made it possible to calculate as fixed costs the charges which had hitherto been dependent on unforeseeable market changes; these strategies served the firms' repeatedly emphasized aim of seeking the greatest possible "market independence" ' (p. 560). As far as downstream industries are concerned, this is also linked to the relative incompleteness of the markets for intermediate inputs in the initial stages of industrial development. More broadly, it can be said that the emphasis put on fixed costs as a factor of risk *reduction* – seen from the quite opposite perspective of the late 1990s – highlights the enormous importance of the changes occurred in the "external" context to explain firm behaviour (see below, sections 1.2 and 1.3).

10 As noted by Carlsson (1996, p. 80), "During the first few decades of the post-war period, firms tended to diversify in order to reduce their exposure risk. This was the golden era of conglomerates". Indeed, the question was clearly perceived by economic analysts since the Golden Age years: in commenting the results of an empirical research by the Federal Trade Commission (*Industrial Concentration and Product Diversification in the Thousand Largest Manufacturing Companies*, US Government Printing Office, 1957), Edwards (1963, p. 119) stresses that "the bigness of the largest enterprises was derived partly from their spread across products and industries, rather than their dominance of single-industry markets".

11 It may be noted that "lateral" integration in this connection applies regardless of its responding to the emergence of scope economies among different activities.

12 The notion of M-form, whose formulation in descriptive terms dates back to Chandler (1966), was set out theoretically by Williamson in two successive contributions (1970 and 1971). Williamson's assumption is that "finite spans of control naturally require that additional hierarchical levels be introduced as the U-form enterprise expands" (1971, p. 346); as this has the effect of reducing the degree of control of managers and amplifying the problems as to the discretional behaviour of each hierarchical level, the firm is induced to adopt a structure (M-form) which is based on breaking down the previous unit into "natural decision units" with substantial decision-making autonomy. The new organization, which is thus made up of "quasi-enterprises" which are subject to a single strategic function, involves relatively lower information requirements (and therefore costs), in addition to a clearer definition of decision-making responsibilities. It has to be recalled in any case that on historical grounds the very first appearance of the M-form actually takes place as early as the 1920s, and coincides with the restructuring of General Motors (see on the point Sloan, 1963, especially chapters 4 and 14).

13 See the review by Hughes and Singh (1980) on this specific point; the importance of mergers in increasing the degree of industrial concentration had already been stressed, with reference to the English experience in the 1950s and 1960s, by Utton (1971).

14 The whole question can be included in the broader issue of the crisis of the so-called Fordist paradigm in many large-scale production types, as has been analysed by Piore and Sabel (1984). It is worthwhile to notice that, according to Piore and Sabel, the effects of mass production on industrial structure did not simply apply to market economies, but also to (formerly) planned economies of Eastern Europe as well as to many developing countries.

15 From here onwards the empirical analysis – unless otherwise specified – refers to a group of six industrial countries comprising France, (West) Germany, Italy, United Kingdom, United States and Japan.

16 As emphasized by Glyn *et al.* (1990, p. 51), "the Golden Age could be regarded as primarily domestically based".

17 The notion of X-inefficiency (first introduced by Leibenstein around the mid-1960s: see the synthesis in Leibenstein 1976) is here meant to recall the reduction of the degree of "in-built" inefficiency occurring when the competition mechanism is at work. See on the point also chapter 2 below.

18 In recent years a number of attempts aimed at (re)founding a theory of firms' boundaries based on *production* prerequisites has been developed, revolving around the notion of "competence" (for a full review of this issue, see Foss and Knudsen, 1996). This overall perspective includes different approaches, more or less centred on the analysis of some "knowledge capital" allowing the firm to achieve better results than its competitors. Competence is seen in this context as an asset which rests with *individuals*, but is really to be found in *organizations*, which are the basic subject of analysis ("firms are seen essentially as repositories of competence", Foss and Knudsen 1996, p. 1). Seen in this way, the possibility for firms to grow both vertically and horizontally is strictly linked to their abilities to develop *from within* (and dynamically) the

necessary knowledge. According to this view both "the death of the conglomerate" and "the need for a return to core business" (p. 3) are attributed to the impossibility to sustain permanent diversification as a long-term corporate strategy.

19　As has been noted by Singh (1997), there is a change from a situation in which "not only were they [the developed economies] subject to international capital controls under the Bretton Woods regime, [but] they also had a plethora of controls, regulations, and other restrictive practices in the domestic product, capital and labour markets" (p. 14), to a situation in which financial liberalization and globalization "create enormous scope for destabilising speculation which in turn leads to high volatility of both monetary and real variables" (p. 24).

20　As has been noted, 'under the Bretton Woods system, foreign exchange risk was borne by the public sector. With that system's collapse, foreign exchange risk was privatized' (Eatwell, 1995, p. 278).

21　'With the events of the 1970s and 1980s ... the resulting volatility of world markets incorporated more elements of genuine uncertainty than "mere" risk' (Carlsson, 1996, p. 80).

22　In this case, the exact opposite occurs of what was said before (see section 11) about the tendency of firms to *increase* their degree of vertical integration when demand is particularly *stable* (that is to say when the downward rigidity of input use is *not* a major problem).

23　In particular, it can be noted that the slowing down of growth in the two more recently industrialized countries (Italy and Japan) is less evident, and that this is associated – in both periods – to a lower variance. As far as the United Kingdom is concerned, variability is simply measured by the standard deviation, owing to the very low value of the average. As can clearly be seen, in this specific case variability is in any case higher than in the second period in absolute terms, and is all the more so in relative terms (that is to say as against the average, which in the second period collapses).

24　In the years following 1973 the conditions which allowed the European countries to catch up with the United States (the leading industrial country in the first post-war phase) gradually disappeared, and at the same time a break in the structural link between output and productivity – according to a Kaldor–Verdoorn view – occurred. This means that the positive impact of technological progress on output growth is reduced, and vice versa. On this issue see Matthews (1982).

25　The fact that output growth is lower than productivity growth may be linked, in the more recent phase and especially in European countries in which the phenomenon is stronger, to the effects of restrictive policies due to need to meet the Maastricht criteria. But in a long-run perspective the crucial difference between the two phases lies in the very uniqueness of the Golden Age: as Kindleberger pointed out as early as in the 1950s (1958, p. 315), "the higher rate of growth has the prospect of slowing down"; that is to say "the Gompertz or S curve applies more or less roughly to growth problems. On only a small portion of it can geometric rates of growth be extrapolated, and then not for long". From this point of view, the endogenous component of the phenomenon re-emerges; we might even go as far as to say that the conditions under which firms' expansion reaches its extreme must be considered absolutely anomalous and therefore cannot be repeated.

26 Indeed, as technological advances gradually allow the setting up of (flexible) manufacturing *systems*, which by their very nature are characterized by large minimum size, the question of indivisibilities comes back again. See for example on the point Mansfield (1992).

27 The point has been widely analysed by Carlsson (1989) and Carlsson *et al.* (1994), according to whom in the US – from the early 1970s to the mid-1980s – those industries most affected by the introduction of numerically controlled machines in production processes underwent a reduction in size (and vice versa). On the broader issue of the relation between firm size and technology see also Dosi (1988).

28 The term "unit" here is intended in the meaning suggested by Austin Robinson (1935); see on this specific point chapter 2 below (sections 2.4 and 2.6).

29 It needs to be stressed in this connection that in more recent years information technologies have spanned across the whole range of the internal activities (functions) of industrial firms. In such a way they have deeply altered the very boundaries of the various activities, making it difficult, in some cases, even to find any boundaries at all between them.

30 A reference can be made to the findings presented as early as the 1940s in a Symposium of the American Economic Association (see, in particular, the paper by Blair, 1948), as well as to many other contributions (see, among others, Pryor 1972, Sargant Florence 1954).

31 The question assumes major relevance in the Italian case, where a peculiarly high proportion of small-scale production units – tied to lagging industrial development – has been a decisive factor in pushing up the growth of the small business sector since the early 1970s (see below, chapters 3 to 5).

32 The perspective suggested by Ms Harrigan appears quite similar to that revealed by Meade's insights (see section 1.1). It also highlights some of the questions raised in chapter 2 of this book (see in particular sections 2.4 and 2.5).

33 For a comprehensive discussion about the methodological issues related to vertical integration measures see Maddigan (1981).

34 The values shown in Figure 1.6 correspond to the (simple) average of the values available at the sectoral level (at input costs – subject to exceptions – and at current prices). Calculations do not include a number of sectors structurally characterized by a limited possibility to break down individual production stages (see table C.2 in Appendix C).

35 A much deeper empirical investigation of the phenomenon analysed here – referring to the four European countries we consider in our analysis – can be found in Arrighetti (1999), whose findings – based upon a different data-set – show a more remarkable fall in the Adelman Index for both Germany and the UK.

36 "Such acquisitions thus reflect the same phenomenon that appears to underlie most friendly takeovers in the 1980s: firms buying other firms or a closely related industry" (p. 44).

37 Properly, the dynamics of self-employment (commonly observed in similar contexts – see, for example, Davis and Henrekson, 1999) measures the

performance of *that* part of self-employment working not only without any employees, but also without resorting to *other* self-employed co-workers. As on the basis of this data the analysis would simply be limited to freelance workers, we consider here the *whole* of self-employment (including co-workers in firms which also make use of employees). Even without considering the problems posed by the lower reliability of estimates concerning freelance self-employed, this figure identifies more precisely (when set against total employment) all those people who work as *entrepreneurs* within firms.

38 Obviously the whole question must be evaluated also taking into account the "pressure" exerted by the very existence of high levels of unemployment on the propensity to self-employment. For a review of this problem see, for example, Meager (1992).

39 When considered in relation to the decreasing trend shown by total unemployment in absolute terms (see section 1.2), such trends show how the creation of new firms accompanying the de-verticalization process is probably linked to spin-off effects (the growing number of self-employed is paralleled by a *decreasing* number of employees).

40 The case which is being made can be highlighted by considering the importance taken on – as the corporate economy reached its climax – by state-owned firms in the Italian case.

41 For a deeper discussion of Simon's analysis about the matter see below, chapter 2.

42 In organizational terms, the above mentioned change recalls the difference made, following Burns and Stalker (1961), by J. Woodward (1965, pp. 23–5) about "mechanistic" systems (characterized by a "well developed command hierarchy through which information filters up and decisions and instructions flow down") as opposed to "organic" ones (which are "more adaptable" and where "jobs lose much of their formal definition"). Most relevant, from the point of view of our work, is the conclusion according to which "mechanistic systems are appropriate to stable conditions and organic systems to conditions of change", for the former are more suitable for standardized production, whereas the latter give a better answer to "one off"-type production, aimed at meeting customers' individual requirements. The question is also recalled by Postan (1967, chapter XI).

2 A Theoretical Framework

1 See here, for instance, Simon (1945), Papandreou (1952), Boulding (1952).

2 For a general overview of the whole question see Hughes (1987).

3 The fact that according to this view there is a difference (organizational slack) between total resources and what are defined as the "total necessary payments" (corresponding to the cost of settling disputes) implies that firms always pay a price for abandoning the optimizing behaviour typical of an agent acting in a perfectly competitive market. Such behaviour is prevented by the fact that, unlike what normally happens in a perfectly competitive market, its decision-making system depends on a *whole series* of individuals, each of whom has *its own* utility function.

4   See the definition given by Alchian and Demsetz (1972); but in a very similar view see also the basic assumptions of the "principal–agent" approach (for all, Jensen and Meckling, 1976).

5   "A workman does not move from Department Y to Department X, because the price in X has risen enough relative to to the price in Y to make the move worthwhile for him. He moves from Y to X because he is ordered to do so" (Coase, 1972, p. 63). It can be noted that such a view appears very close to Marx's analysis (see Putterman, 1986); a very similar point of view can also be found in D. Robertson (1928).

6   Of course, growth may nonetheless bring about lower costs simply as a consequence of the possible emergence of *scope* economies.

7   See Cyert and March (1963).

8   From our point of view, a general formulation of this principle (see, for instance, Williamson, 1993) may be that insofar as contracts cannot escape from incompleteness, opportunistic behaviour – as it is allowed by bounded rationality – makes way for vertical integration, so as to put transactions under the control of the entrepreneur's authority. The higher assets' specificity (that is, the degree in which parties are mutually dependent for their investments), the stronger the incentive to integrate.

9   The condition for both situations (the integrated versus the non-integrated "multi-firm" economy) to be indifferent on "technical" grounds would be that the total amount of inputs (of costs) required for producing a given output were the same. For *overall* costs to be identical in the two situations, the costs of transacting among (small) decentralized agents should also equal the costs borne by the integrated firm for "transferring" intermediate inputs internally across the different stages of production. Transacting costs include the search for information (below, section 2.4) and the sum of the mark-ups which (small) firms in the "intermediate" phases of the production chain add to their unit costs. The tightening of competiton, in this context, may tend to squeeze "intermediate" firms' mark-up towards zero (the market option involves the absence of any market power), but it can hardly contribute to determine any differences between the two systems of production as it relates to "technical" costs: *all* firms, be they vertically dis-integrated or not, are pushed to minimize costs. On the other hand, increasing market turbulence raises the costs for gathering information. In a static perspective, unless exceptional changes on technological grounds are admitted (leading to higher technical efficiency for smaller-scale plants), "economizing" will produce fairly similar results in both cases. The only relevant effect which vertical dis-integration may involve could stem – more or less according to some "Stiglerian" view – from the existence of *dynamic* economies arising from growing *specialization* (as this is brought about by the sheer decomposition of the production process). But this should in turn require a quite substantial *expansion* of the market: however, whereas it is certainly true that *some* markets for products have experienced a strong expansion, on average the "fall" in the size of firms has been paralleled, as we have seen, by the ending of the Golden Age, that is by a sharp reduction (jointly with rising average volatility) in the output rate of growth of the major industrial economies.

10   The authors explicitly refer to works by Powell (1990) and Loasby (1994).

11   As Robinson's view is specifically concerned, things are obviously to be considered as more complex. See in particular section 2.4 below and section 5.1 in chapter 5.

12   'A mythical visitor from Mars, not having been apprised of the centrality of markets and contracts, might find the new institutional economics rather astonishing. (...) For almost all of the inhabitants would be employees, hence inside the firm boundaries [,] organizations would be the dominant feature of the landscape. (...) Our visitor might be surprised to hear the structure called a market economy. "Wouldn't 'organizational economy' be the more appropriate term?" it might ask' (Simon, 1991, p. 28).

13   From this point of view, wages reflect the willingness of employees to "bear the brunt of ... uncertainty as to what actions will be chosen".

14   This reflects a basic scepticism about the possibility of controlling the behaviour of employees through enforcement mechanisms (such as those envisaged in principal–agent models), due to the huge amount of resources that would be required for a similar purpose (on this point see also Chang and Singh, 1997). More generally, this has to do with a view according to which "the attempts of the new institutional economics to explain organizational behaviour solely in terms of agency, asymmetric information, transaction costs, opportunism and other concepts drawn from neoclassical economics ignore key organizational mechanisms like authority, identification, and coordination and hence are seriously incomplete" (Simon, 1991, p. 42).

15   Such a way of looking at organizational behaviour seems to get close to Ouchi's (1980) treatment of the role of "clans" (indeed, Ouchi explicitly refers to Simon's 1945 book), according to which within an organization the incongruence among the objectives of different agents and ambiguity in performance evaluation can be minimized by the "organic solidarity" stemming, as a "form of mediation", from the unavoidable dependence of individuals on each other.

16   This seems to be especially relevant in view of the fact that, as we know, the tendency to reducing organizational complexity (to reducing size) has been quite intense in large companies, where such principles had played a very important role in the course of the Golden Age of industrial development.

17   A similar point may be raised starting from the perspective of the relationship between "formal" and "real" authority inside organizations. As is suggested – even if in a quite different context than ours – by Aghion and Tirole (1997), who explicity refer to Max Weber, it can be said that the ownership of an asset does not necessarily confer *real* authority, in terms of an effective control over decisions. This view – which can be considered quite at odds with the hypotheses put forth, for example, by theorists like Hart and Moore (1990) – hinges upon the principle that the administrative staff of a bureaucracy may exert *in its turn* a quite substantial control over the "bureaucratic machinery", even in the absence of any ownership of (non-human) means of production. The key role in this context is played by asymmetric information: "formal" authority can prevail *only* when owners ("principals") have adequate information about the projects which are proposed by subordinates ("agents"). An important point here is that "a principal who is overloaded with too many activities ... and therefore has little time to acquire the relevant information on each activity loses effective control and involuntarily

endorses many sub-optimal projects" (Aghion and Tirole, p. 3); from the point of view of the present work this means that as far as the amount of "relevant" information gets greater because of the growing complexity of the problems to be taken under control (for instance, as a consequence of rising uncertainty), the efficiency of organizations may tend to fall. This specific issue is at the root of the analysis developed in section 2.4 below.

18 Malmgren calls this kind of information "controlled information"; Richardson terms it 'technical information'.

19 Indeed, "provided its efficiency ... in controlling its primary data does not fall" (Malmgren, 1961, p. 416).

20 It has to be stressed in this connection that also the *overall costs* of gathering information may anyway rise even in the face of *falling unit* (per message) costs, when the number of messages rises. And this is just what actually happens, since firms have now to face an often overwhelming *amount* of messages, which need more and more resources simply to be *processed*.

21 A fairly similar point can be found in Arrow (1984, p. 145), when observing that the strongest constraint in the acquisition of information "is the limitation on the ability of any individual [of the human mind] to process information".

22 From this point of view it can be said that the rate of development of internal "coordinating ability" affects the *speed* at which firms can expand. A wider analysis of the whole question can be found in Traù (1996).

23 The whole question raised above is paid more specific attention in chapter 5 (section 5.1.2).

24 Properly, in this connection we have to take into account that the managerial role does not simply coincide with *control* (managers are also required to innovate, to find new market opportunities and so on). And, indeed, the lack of such capabilities appears to be the most significant force acting against new (small) firms' expansion.

25 For a proper discussion about the whole matter see for instance Brewer (1994, ch. 4).

26 "The appropriate support for a physical structure is a perfect diagram of the forces tending to destroy it" (Haire, 1959, p. 276). Or, in more "analogical" terms, "a deer cannot grow as big as an elephant and still look like a deer; it has to look (something) like an elephant to support the elephant mass" (p. 274).

27 A similar point is raised by Radner (1992), who shows how the secular rise in the size of US firms since 1900 has been paralleled by a regular increase in the share of the labour force devoted to "managing" activities (broadly defined as those where people are involved in "figuring out what to do, in contrast to do it", p. 1387).

28 This is also partially due to the fact that it is not that easy to simply "buy" resources from outside, because of the existence of something like a Penrose constraint ("efficient" organizational resources can only ripen *inside* the firm). Insofar as it acts on the "speed" of the growth process (see section 2.4.2), this specific effect entails some lag in the rhythm of expansion of internal input endowments with respect to the rise of coordination costs. As Marris (1964) puts it, "organisation must be created where none existed before, recruits must be found, new tasks undertaken and new delegation-patterns developed.

It is axiomatic that such planning can only be undertaken by existing members. If an organisation is to remain efficient, it cannot possibly expand at an indefinitely rapid rate merely by infinitely rapid recruitment" (p. 114).

29 The market price of externalized inputs may be lower or *equal* to the cost of producing them internally.

30 As we saw in chapter 1, this seems not to be true for Japan (see Figure 1.5), with respect to which, however, we do not have at disposal data about *firms*.

31 Macroeconomic changes have to be considered in turn as endogenous with respect to the forces leading to the exhausting of the Golden Age.

32 In other words, the firm cannot absorb rising unit costs (involved by the passage from π_1 to π_2) by rising output prices.

33 In a rather similar perspective the relationship between information costs and the internal organization of firms (viewed in its turn as closely related to size) has been recently addressed on theoretical grounds by Casson (1996). Starting from the premise that "organisational structure can be explained as the outcome of attempts to minimise information costs", Casson shows that smaller firms will "specialise" in volatile environments (more precisely, in environments "which have a single major source" of volatility), whereas larger ones will tend to operate in relatively stable environments (i.e. those in which "no source of volatility is sufficiently large to dominate the others"). This is linked to the fact that small units rely less than large enterprises on complex routine procedures (which require a "consultative management style"), and are on the contrary characterized by an "autocratic" style of management, grounded upon the belief that the entrepreneur possesses "the key information relevant to the decision" (pp. 329–30).

34 It seems important to stress here that an excess of *entrepreneurial* supply (in the sense suggested by Tuck) may be quite compatible with an overall shortage of *managerial* resources.

3 Empirical Analysis I: Employment Shares and Absolute Employment Growth at the Size Level for Firms and Establishments: Six Industrial Countries in Two Different Phases of Industrial Development

1 This analysis culminated in the proposition – by Sabel and others – of the model of "flexible specialization". See, in particular, Piore and Sabel (1984). A (very) critical reconsideration of the whole matter can be found in Landes (1984); an attempt to envisage the question within the framework of a wider theory of competitive adaption can be found in Best (1990).

2 In terms of original calculations, the OECD analysis provided evidence, with reference to various industrial countries, about the trend of manufacturing employment shares in four size classes, drawn from various sources. The report also surveyed available statistical evidence about the impact of firm entries and exits on net job creation.

3 The analysis comprises the G7 Group with the exception of Canada – that is, the four largest European economies, United States and Japan. Each country is paid specific attention in a chapter of the book; overall results are illustrated in a synthesis by the editors.

4   It has to be noticed in this respect that the German data exclude firms with less than 20 employees.

5   It may be added in this connection – as the authors themselves point out – that an increase in employment, even in absolute numbers, says nothing about the *output* weight of small units, for it may simply reflect a change in production techniques (a shift along the production function) for any given output level. The literature on the subject, nonetheless, seems to provide some evidence about the existence of a positive relationship between employment and output trends (especially as it concerns the "other side" of the question, that is the falling output weight of *large* businesses). See on the point Dunne and Hughes (1992) and Henley (1994) as to the British case, and Traù (1994) about the three other large European countries included in the above mentioned analysis (namely France, Germany and Italy), in addition to the UK.

6   Relevant problems affect, in particular, German data (where data referring to years prior to 1976 cannot be compared to those referring to later years, owing to differing boundaries of the population and to the absence of information about firms with fewer than 20 employees), Japan (where data are taken from the OECD 1985 Report, which in turn did not take them from Business Censuses, but simply from Labour Force Surveys series), France (where data are indirectly drawn from the reconstruction made by Didier and Malinvaud, 1969 and Didier, 1982). See on this point also the criticisms by Storey (1994, chapter 2).

7   Among the few attempts to provide evidence about the role played by the small business sector in developing countries we can recall here the Annual Conferences held by the International Council for Small Business (as an example, see with reference to Asian emerging economies the papers presented at the Conference held in Naples in June 1998).

8   See in this respect Schwalbach (1994), who analyses (for the whole economy) the lowering of average size in 12 European countries in the first half of the 1980s, Traù (1994), who observes the phenomenon over the whole 1980s, and Acs and Audretsch (1993), who extend the analysis to some countries from Eastern Europe. On the whole, such studies confirm – as to the areas and periods they refer to – the existence of an overall employment shift towards smaller-sized units.

9   See among others, apart from the study by Marsden included in the ILO Research (chapter 6), Stanworth and Gray (1991), Dunne and Hughes (1992), Hughes (1993), Robson and Gallagher (1994), Henley (1994), and the many contributions by Storey (for a synthesis see Storey 1994, in particular chapter 2). Indeed, the attention paid to the role played by the small business sector can be traced back to the late 1960s, when the so-called Bolton Report was published (see Bolton, 1971). Obviously, at that time the findings of the report (even if they were cautious about future developments) could not but testify the falling importance the small business sector was then experiencing: "The small firm sector is in a state of long-term decline, both in size and in its share of economic activity" (Bolton, 1971, p. 342).

10 In the study by Henley (1994) such evidence is buttressed by other evidence showing a fall, over the period 1980–87, in concentration measured on a gross output (sales) basis.

11 The degree of coverage of the population shows a sharp upturn in 1984, due to methodological changes in the logic of data collection (this is especially true below the threshold of nine employees). This problem is enhanced by other problems pertaining to the existence of discontinuities in sectoral boundaries, in particular within manufacturing. See anyway on this point Dunne and Hughes (1992), and the Appendix A at the end of this book.

12 See among others Fritsch (1993), Schwalbach (1994), Stockmann and Leicht (1994).

13 See Sengenberger *et al.* (1990, chapter 3). Even more than the limited amount of information provided in the paper what has to be stressed here is the rather baffling assertion by the author that – in the face of a spectacular stability in the employment shares of small firms and establishments over the whole period considered – "employment in small and medium-sized establishments with fewer than 200 employees showed a considerable increase in the 1970s", p. 115).

14 Actually, even the study by Amadieu in the ILO Research (see Sengenberger *et al.*, 1990, chapter 2) simply collects data from these previous studies, so that on empirical grounds the phenomenon does not extend beyond 1981.

15 It has to be stressed that this hypothesis – frequently addressed by literature – is in conflict with the view according to which the small business sector is *structurally* characterized by a higher degree of "flexibility" with respect to exogenous shocks, *be they positive or negative* (see on this point the model suggested by Mills and Schumann, 1985, and, for a more recent contribution relative to the Italian case, Ferrando and Ganoulis, 1999).

16 Main references may include Barca (1985), Contini and Revelli (1992), Traù (1997 and 1998). A synthesis of some of the issues addressed in Contini and Revelli (1992) can be found in an English-language version in Contini (1984); the above mentioned papers by Traù summarize broader evidence provided in wider works published in Italian.

17 In Italy business censuses are taken every ten years, in the first year of any decade.

18 Properly, as we will more widely show below, direct comparisons between Italy and Japan are actually thwarted by the lack of data about *firms* for the latter; in this connection also see Appendix A.

19 See Sengenberger *et al.* (1990, ch. 5).

20 Data refer in this case to firms; for we are here below the threshold of 100 employees, the difference with establishments should not be decisive.

21 See on this point below, section 3.4.

22 See again Sengenberger *et al.* (1990, ch. 7).

23 The sectoral breakdown of the data-set broadly corresponds to the three Isic (Rev. 2) digits. Adaptions are made in order to make comparisons with the (OECD) Stan data-base possible.

24 The group includes, other than small economies such as Luxembourg and the Nederlands, even Liechtenstein.

25 Data contained in the report come – depending on the countries they refer to – from information drawn both from Census data and from surveys referring to (wider or narrower) firm sets belonging to the whole population (this also involves the wide use of estimation about size bands not covered by original data). As a consequence, "the degree of harmonisation of the

national data sets received by Eurostat is such that direct comparisons between countries can only be made in a very limited number of cases". (...) "For example, the unit used, the coverage by sector and/or size and the definition of a variable may vary from one country to another" (Eurostat, 1994, vol. 2, p. 4).

26   The data-set at the heart of the analysis by Ehrlich (1985) is published in Ehrlich *et al.* (1982).

27   This means that the fall in average size is strongly affected by a diminishing employment weight of smaller establishments (which, in itself, is a structural feature of the early phases of the industrialization process).

28   Simply, in this case 'the administrative requirements of a centralized economic control system played a dominant role. This system cannot function efficiently on the basis of small-scale, autonomous economic units; the command of relatively small enterprises by plan directives became more and more difficult' (Ehrlich, 1985, p. 294).

29   German data have been collected up to 1990. From this point of view the belief has prevailed that the collapse of former DDR in Western Germany has involved a *structural* difference in nature of the new entity with respect to BRD, such to make any comparison over time basically meaningless.

30   It is *extremely* important to stress that, in particular as it concerns *firms*, the definitions adopted by National Statistical Systems (Business Censuses) show important cross-country differences. This basic heterogeneity suggests not to rely too much on cross-country comparisons referring to *levels* (this is very much true even in the case of "officially" harmonized data such as those provided, for example, in *Enterprises in Europe*, see Appendix A); nevertheless this problem does not affect intertemporal comparisons within any given country – i.e. the main object of our analysis.

31   Calculations have been replied excluding from the first size band firms with fewer than ten employees (that is, those included in the range more subject to discontinuities in the business register series); the basic absence of differences in results between the two subsets leads us in this case to evaluate this effect as negligible. The problem represented by business registers discontinuities, anyway, has to be borne in mind in the following of this analysis, in particular as it relates to the United Kingdom, where it assumes special relevance. This question is addressed on general grounds in Appendix A, and pointed out in following chapters whenever it may involve any effects on empirical results.

32   In the German case differences in the coverage of population across time as it concerns artisan units (excluded in 1962, included in 1990, available in both versions in 1977) have required – in this graph as well as in following ones – two different calculations, so as to make possible comparisons across both periods.

33   The cross-references between Isic codes and industrial activities are contained in Appendix C.

34   The question of the behaviour of firms as compared to plants is paid specific attention in chapter 5.

35   See again on this point Appendix A.

36   For the same reasons recalled above German data referring to the 1970s are presented in two distinct versions (either including or excluding artisan firms).

37 In Table 3.1 the sectoral breakdown is lower than in Figure 3.2 owing to the
    need to compare different countries.
38 It is important to stress here that comparisons among the changes showed in
    figures can be made only *within* a given country, because the number of years
    referring to each phase differs according to individual countries.
39 The term "contribution" here simply refers to the sign in the observed
    variation.
40 As a matter of evidence, medium-sized firms (those with 100 to 500 employees)
    do not play such a role as well.
41 As to Germany, employment falls above the threshold corresponding to 500
    employees since years *preceding* 1977 – which involves a fall in total manu-
    facturing employment. This seems not obvious; but it is consistent with data
    provided by National Accounts (OECD source), which also show a certain
    reduction in the number of employees in the period involved.

4 Empirical Analysis II: The Number of Business Units and their Average Size over the Long Run: Models of Industrial Development

1 Properly, the possibility of "transitions" *internal* to each size interval also
   have to be taken into account in this connection.
2 This way of approaching the question can also help us to specify the relationship between the changes occurring in the shares of employment and those
   which occur in the shares of *firms* – simply, the latter do *involve* the former,
   that is on the one side firms' transition across size classes takes place through
   the "hiring or firing" of workforce; on the other firms' entries (exits) coincide
   with the entries (exits) of their employees.The difference between considering employment as against firms merely boils down to taking into account
   the actual "weight", in economic terms, of the observed business units.
3 Under the threshold corresponding to ten employees jumps in business registers make it often quite difficult to distinguish changes in the number of
   existing units from discontinuities in the degree of coverage of the population. Therefore, some calculations hereafter are also provided with reference
   to the population of units with more than ten employees only.
4 Data referring to Japan exclude the Food and Tobacco industries (Isic codes
   311 to 314), due to their rather anomalous behaviour in the "Restructuring"
   years (when they are characterized by a sharp rise in their average size vis à vis
   a general fall in size in *all* other industries). The point here is that the single
   value corresponding to codes 311–314, owing to their very high weight in
   terms of employment, would completely offset the opposite dynamics of
   other industries, thereby altering quite sharply the overall trend for the manufacturing sector as a whole. See for a detailed view Figures 4.1 and 4.2 below.
5 See section 4.3 below and Appendix A.
6 Sectors have been aggregated in both figures in order to achieve a common
   breakdown for different countries (the original national breakdowns having
   been heterogeneous). Some differences in sectoral breakdown persist in figures
   referring to firms with respect to those referring to plants.

7   This is at the very root of the rapid response of Italian industry to the changing "competitive environment" after the Golden Age came to an end, which led to a noticeable increase in the economic weight of small businesses in the manufacturing sector (see on this point in particular Arrighetti, 1999). It has also to be clarified that such a trend is not to be considered at variance with our findings about the evolution of employment shares at the size-class level (see Figure 3.2d in chapter 3). In this respect Figure 4.1 simply shows that the average *scale* at which manufacturing activities were performed was *already* falling in many industries in the Golden Age years, even in the face of a *relative* reduction in the contribution smaller-sized firms gave to employment (which can be more than offset by a parallel decrease in the average size of units belonging to the – larger – size classes increasing their employment shares).

8   Section 4.4.3 shows that in the Golden Age years average size for firms up to 100 employees (micro-firms *included*) did *rise*; this means that increases in size actually occurred *below* the threshold of 10 employees. As we will argue, this has much to do with the backwardness of the Italian industrialization process as late as the 1960s, involving a quite large weight of micro-units which still had to grow to achieve the minimum efficient size.

9   Establishments' behaviour in Italy is in such respect akin to the observed trends for firms.

10   Figure 4.3 refers to units with more than ten employees, so as to compare "technical" units belonging to that part of the industrial system which should be relatively independent of national specificities as it regards size structure. When performed with reference to the whole size distribution, the overall tendency outlined above appears less clear-cut (in a number of industries variance flattens), but in the majority of cases it results confirmed.

11   With respect to more recent years, the question is dealt with – even if simply referring to *firms* – in a paper by Geroski and Gugler (2001), who show the absence of any convergence in size within European manufacturing to the mid-1990s.

12   Figures referring to the United Kingdom raise some relevant questions as to their statistical reliability. These problems stem from the rather muddled organization of business registers in the UK, and especially from the important changes occurring over time in data collection as well as in the definition of the variables included in business censuses (see on the point Appendix A). Whilst on the whole data referring to average size (as well as those relative to *employment* shares) involve in themselves some sorts of compensation of possible jumps in the coverage of the entire population of business units, data referring to the *number* of such units may show quite anomalous changes from time to time (especially with regard to the first historical phase analysed here). All empirical evidence provided in this secion has to be evaluated in the light of these basic problems; as it happens in Figure 4.4, in some cases the calculations exclude UK figures.

13   The question has some relevance on theoretical grounds; see on this point chapter 2 (section 2.3).

14   As mentioned above (see note 12), Table 4.4 does not include UK figures.

15 It is worth noting that at the size-class level changes in the number of firms over time may involve changes in firm size *in addition* to entries and exits relative to the *whole* size distribution.

16 As we have seen, Japanese data are only available for establishments.

17 On the other hand, the very coincidence itself, in the "Restructuring" phase, of a growing number of firms and a general fall in their average size suggests that for the most part the wider boundaries of the population of business units are due to entries of new *small* ones.

18 It is worth recalling here what we observed in section 4.2.2 above about the tendency of average size to decrease in some Italian industries even during the Golden Age period.

5 Firms versus Plants: a Closer Examination of their Different Behaviour in the Face of Structural Change

1 See Penrose (1980, p. 13).

2 This does not necessarily mean that changes depending on the latter are necessarily greater than those depending on the former.

3 As is well known, even the problem of the "simple" relationship between scale and returns, since Sraffa's (1926) attack on the Marshallian tradition, is still far from being resolved. Even if the question as to what extent technological factors do actually affect (plant) size goes far beyond the boundaries of this work, we can recall here the basic inconclusiveness of the debate about the shape of long-run cost functions: on both theoretical and empirical grounds no clear-cut conclusion about the existence of a precise functional relation (of any kind) between size and returns can be found in the current literature (an attempt to synthesize the whole question can be found in Traù, 1996). This leads in turn to a "looseness" in any hypotheses about the actual impact of changes in available technology on plant size (that is, on the economic advantages of investing in large as opposed to small plants, or vice versa).

4 The same can be said as it relates to any differences across countries in the observed trends in plant size.

5 As we recalled in chapter 1, the question was explicitly addressed in a symposium of the American Economic Association in the late 1940s. On that occasion Blair (1948) wrote that "as a result of new decentralizing techniques in the field of power, material, machinery and transportation, technology is now tending to promote a smaller, than a larger scale of operations" (p. 151). A similar view was set forth just a few years later by Jewkes (1952), arguing that "we need not assume that the technical equipment of industry consists of large and indivisible blocks. If that were true the variety in the size of factories would not be so great as it actually is. (...) The equipment of industry is still broken up into a large number of relatively small pieces, and from the technical point of view might perhaps, without loss, be broken up further" (p. 251).

6 This question can also be viewed in the light of what has been observed in chapter 3 about the long-run behaviour of absolute employment levels in both small plants and small firms (i.e. largely the same thing): the overall

stability of such levels – as opposed to the "rise and fall" of employment in *large* units – testifies in itself that some *economic* convenience of small-scale *production* has been *constantly* at work over all phases of industrial development.

7   See on this specific point chapter 2.

8   It can be noted that this is, in fact, what most contributions on the subject – clearly influenced by a view which attributes to the firm the role of a simple production function – seem to imply (see, for example, Stigler 1939, Mills and Schumann 1985, Carlsson 1989).

9   This seems to have been especially true in the Italian experience, where external administrative functions have become the rule in the organization of economic activity in a large part of the industrial sector.

10   As has been observed in chapter 2, the key point here is that uncertainty means that the firm (given its overall size) has to process a larger *amount* of relevant information; the question as to the *cost* of such information comes in a sense afterwards, and has a less significant role.

11   As to the latter, it could even be hypothesized that technology might have played no role at all, inasmuch as organizations can grow on their own even in the face of a fall in the size of each of their constitutive elements (provided their overall *number* grows accordingly).

12   It needs to be stressed, in this respect, that taking this view would mean assuming the working at a microeconomic level of macroeconomic "laws" such as those described by Kaldor (1966) and Baumol (1967). This cannot be considered to be straightforward, for – as is well known – the mechanisms explaining the setting up of *dynamic* increasing returns in those theories act through the *aggregate* behaviour of agents.

13   Measurement issues are paid explicit attention in Appendix B at the end of this book.

14   See on this point chapter 3.

15   As we have said repeatedly, this has to be related to the degree of "maturity" of American industry as compared to the Italian.

16   A similar view about the role played by "administrative" economies as opposed to "production" ones, has been recently raised by Pryor (2001), who suggests comparing the changes in number of establishments as against firms – through the ratio of the former to the latter – in order to infer the existence of any difference in their trend, for "the costs of production are more often associated with establishments, while the costs of organization are tied to the firm as a whole" (p. 368). Unlike what has repeatedly been stressed in these pages both on theoretical and empirical grounds, however (see in particular chapters 2 and 4), Pryor argues that investment in information technologies may have *lowered* coordination costs, having made an *increase* in the average size of firms possible due to a higher ability to manage more establishments than before. On empirical grounds, anyway, Pryor's findings – starting from similar methodological premises – are similar to those provided in Figure 5.3: for those firms with more than 99 employees, the ratio of plants to firms in the entire private sector (excluding agriculture) presents a relatively low value at the beginning of the 1960s (9.8 per cent), reaches a peak in the early 1980s (15.3 per cent) and falls to 12.5 per cent in 1997.

17 In such case German 1960s data may be directly compared with data referring to later years, since the lack of information about small artisan firms for
years following 1977 only affects those units with fewer than 20 employees.

18 Positive values of OE correspond to *(a)* positive variations in firm size coupled with variations in plant size which are either negative or positive and
lower; *(b)* negative variations in firm size coupled with variations in plant
size which are both negative and lower. Negative values of OE correspond to
(a) negative variations in firm size coupled with variations in plant size
which are either positive or negative and greater; *(b)* positive variations in
firm size coupled with variations in plant size which are both positive and
greater.

19 This has obviously to be evaluated in the light of the fact that in the US case
the "firm" is defined in a somewhat broader sense than it is in the case of
Germany and Italy.

6 Concluding Remarks

1 Incidentally, it can be noted that the basic unpredictability of this last
question has much to do with the policies imposed by international institutions upon developing countries – traditionally encouraging patterns of
development that are relatively intensive in large-scale organizations, vis à
vis a structural scarcity of large-scale organizational capacity. On this specific
point see an illuminating contribution by Olson (1987). For a broader view
on the topic also see the May 2001 Special Issue of the *Cambridge Journal of
Economics* on African Economic Development (vol. 25, no. 3).

2 As to the specific need for distinguishing between "real" and "financial" size
aspects (generally treated in literature in a quite confusing way), a basic reference can be found in Marx's distinction between industrial *concentration* (pertaining to the organization of *production*) and *centralization*, which, according
to Marx, refers to the financial property of economic units: "centralization
may result from a mere change in the distribution of already existing capitals,
from a simple alteration in the quantitative grouping of the component parts
of the social capital" (Marx, 1977, vol. 1, chapter 25, p. 779).

3 Empirical evidence shows quite clearly that both retailing and finance have
been characterized over recent years by a strong tendency towards concentration (generally reflecting the existence of increasing returns) – that is, just
the opposite of what our empirical analysis has revealed with reference to
manufacturing activities.

4 See, for example, on this point the contributions collected in Colombo (1998).

Appendix A: Building a New Data-Set on Industrial Structure: Six Industrial Countries from the Early 1960s to the Mid-1990s[1]

1 The data-set described in this Appendix was constructed between 1998 and
2000 by a research group formed by Annalisa Armanni, Anita Guelfi,
Raffaella Sadun and Fabrizio Traù. All members of the group have worked in

close cooperation in the course of the period over which the data-set has been planned and implemented. The final draft of this section (Appendix A) has been written by Anita Guelfi and Raffaella Sadun.

2   Actually, Eurostat provides a common definition of "enterprise" which should be adopted by each single country. However, this definition is very general and does not really force the national statistical offices to improve the degree of harmonization of required statistics which is, therefore, very poor.

3   Some countries do include self-employment, some others do not.

4   See Eurostat (1994), vol. 2, p. 4.

5   It also provides data on gross value-added and output, which are not considered in the present research project.

6   See section A.3 below.

7   The six countries are the same as those analysed in the wider empirical analysis carried out at the international level previous to this work (see Sengenberger *et al.*, 1990 – referred to in the text as ILO Research).

8   In the case of Italy, data from 1971 onward have been directly provided by the National Institute of Statistics.

9   This was the case for French firms and US establishments in 1977. After careful verification, some changes have been introduced in the original data-set as refers to French employment in the smallest firms. These data looking unrealistic, they have been replaced with specific estimates. No adjustment was required for US data.

10   With the sole exception of the 1963 Census.

11   Actually, some statistics on firms have also been compiled in Japan since 1960. These data are derived from the establishment census, but the way data are aggregated to obtain firm statistics looks particularly unreliable and unclear. For further details, see Guelfi and Traù (1999, p. 94).

12   For these countries, the definition of *enterprise* appears roughly consistent with that provided by Eurostat, according to which: "The enterprise is the smallest combination of legal units that is an organisational unit producing goods or services, which benefits of a certain degree of autonomy in decision-making, especially for the allocation of its current resources. An enterprise carries out one or more activities at one or more locations. An enterprise may be a sole legal unit" (Eurostat, 1994, vol. II, p. 5).

13   Note, however, that the concept of *establishment* does not coincide with that of *local unit*. Indeed: "The industrial establishment is, ideally, an economic unit which engages, under a single ownership or control, in one or predominantly one kind of industrial activity at a single location ... The local unit comprises all the industrial activities carried on under a single ownership or control at a single location; it differs from the establishment in that nothing is said about the range of those activities" (United Nations, 1963, p. 14).

14   The data cross-check consists in a comparison between the total (i.e. relative to the entire manufacturing industry) actual value of each size class and the total value obtained after the estimation of missing data. Such procedures can be applied only if the distribution of the values relative to the entire manufacturing industry follows the predefined size-class criteria. Whenever a difference emerges between actual and estimated totals, an iterative procedure takes place, according to which the values are adjusted within single sectors.

Appendix B: Measuring Firm Size

1 Indeed, studies of such a kind are normally carried out by making use of all sorts of size measures; anybody having had anything to do with them is aware of how difficult it actually is trying to get a synthetic view of their empirical findings.

2 One of the studies mentioned in our survey of empirical research (namely that of van Ark and Monnikhof, 1996, see chapter 3 above) goes as far as publishing some estimation of (both gross and net) output values at the size-class level, with reference to five of the six countries analysed in this book (data refer to firms or establishments alternatively, according to source availability). Our view is that this attempt has to be considered overly ambitious as far as a fairly sound reliability of basic data has to be guaranteed, insofar as the collection of output data calls for an extremely wide use of estimation procedures, especially as it concerns smaller size classes.

3 As we have seen in chapters 3 and 4 in relation to employment, in the two historical periods covered by our analysis, two quite different total employment trends in absolute numbers can be observed (in almost all countries, a growth during the course of the Golden Age and a decrease in the "Restructuring" period).

4 Relevant discontinuities in series make it almost impossible to obtain reliable comparisons with data referring to subsequent years. In the present case, data do not refer to a panel, but simply to the population of firms with more than 20 employees in Italian manufacturing as it results from Business Registers in each year.

References

Acs, Z.J., and Audretsch, D.B. (1990), Small Firms in the 1990s, in Z.J. Acs and D.B. Audretsch (eds), *The Economics of Small Firms: a European Challenge*, Dordrecht, Kluwer.

Acs, Z.J., and Audretsch, D.B. (eds) (1993), *Small Firms and Entrepreneurship: an East–West Perspective*, Cambridge, Cambridge University Press.

Aghion, F., and Tirole, J. (1997), Formal and Real Authority in Organizations, *Journal of Political Economy*, 105 (1), 1–29.

Alchian, A., and Demsetz, H. (1972), Production, Information Costs, and Economic Organization, *American Economic Review*, 62 (5), 777–95.

Arrighetti, A. (1999), Integrazione verticale in Italia e in Europa: tendenze e ipotesi interpretative [English translation available on request], in F. Traù (ed.), *La "questione dimensionale" nell'industria italiana*, Bologna, Il Mulino.

Arrow, K.J. (1984), Information and Economic Behavior, in *Collected Papers of K.J. Arrow, vol. 4: The Economics of Information*, Oxford, Basil Blackwell.

Baldwin, J.R. (1998), Were Small Producers the Engine of Growth in the Canadian Manufacturing Sector in the 1980s?, *Small Business Economics*, 10 (4), 349–64.

Barca, F. (1985), Tendenze della Struttura Dimensionale dell'Industria Italiana: una Verifica Empirica del "Modello di Specializzazione Flessibile", *Politica Economica*, 1 (1), 71–109.

Baumol, W.J. (1967), Macroeconomics of Unbalanced Growth: the Anatomy of Urban Crisis, *American Economic Review*, 62 (3), 415–26.

Berle, A.A., and Means, G.C. (1932), *The Modern Corporation and Private Property*, New York, The Macmillan Company.

Best, M.H. (1990), *The New Competition: Institutions of Industrial Restructuring*, Oxford, Polity Press.

Bhagat, S., Shleifer, A., and Vishny, R.W. (1990), Hostile Takeovers in the 1980s: the Return to Corporate Specialization, *Brookings Papers on Economic Activity (Microeconomics, Special Issue)*.

Blair, J.M. (1948), Technology and Size, *American Economic Review*, Papers & Proceedings, 38 (2), 121–52.

Board of Trade (1969), *Report on the Census of Production 1963*, London, HMSO.

Bolton, J.E. (1971), *Report of the Committee of Inquiry on Small Firms*, London, HMSO.

Boulding, K.E. (1952), Implications for General Economics of More Realistic Theories of the Firm, *American Economic Review*, 42 (2), 35–44.

Boulding, K.E. (1958), *The Skills of the Economist*, London, Hamish Hamilton.

Brewer, R. (1994), *The Science of Ecology*, Austin, TX, Harcourt Brace.

Buiter, W., Lago, R., and Stern, N. (1997), Enterprise Performance and Macroeconomic Control, *Banca Nazionale del Lavoro Quarterly Review*, 50 (200), 3–22.

Bureau of Statistics (various years), *Establishment Census of Japan, 1960, 1975*, Tokyo, Office of the Prime Minister.

Burns, T., and Stalker, G.M. (1961), *The Management of Innovation*, London, Tavistock.

Central Statistical Office Business Monitor (various years), *Report of the Census of Production*, PA 1002, London, HMSO.

Central Statistical Office Business Monitor (various years), *Report of the Census of Production*, PA 1003, London, HMSO.

Carlsson, B. (1989a), Flexibility and the Theory of the Firm, *International Journal of Industrial Organization*, 7 (2), 179–203.

Carlsson, B. (1989b), The Evolution of Manufacturing Technology and Its Impact on Industrial Structure: an International Study, *Small Business Economics*, 1 (1), 21–37.

Carlsson, B. (1996), Small Business, Flexible Technology and Industrial Dynamics, in P.H. Admiraal (ed.), *Small Business in the Modern Economy*, Oxford, Basil Blackwell.

Carlsson, B., Audretsch, D.B., and Acs, Z.J. (1994), Flexible Technology and Plant Size in U.S. Manufacturing and Metalworking Industries, *International Journal of Industrial Organization*, 12 (3), 359–72.

Carlton, D.W. (1979), Vertical Integration in Competitive Markets Under Uncertainty, *Journal of Industrial Economics*, 27 (3), 189–209.

Carree, M., and Thurik, R. (1991), Recent Developments in the Dutch Firm-Size Distribution, *Small Business Economics*, 3 (4), 261–8.

Casson, M. (1991), *The Economics of Business Culture*, New York, Oxford University Press.

Casson, M. (1996), The Comparative Organisation of Large and Small Firms: an Information Cost Approach, *Small Business Economics*, 8 (5), 329–45.

Chandler, A.D. (1966), *Strategy and Structure: Chapters in the History of the Industrial Enterprise*, Cambridge, MA, MIT Press.

Chandler, A.D. (1978), United States, in P. Mathias and M.M. Postan (eds), *Cambridge Economic History of Europe, Vol. VII (The Industrial Economies. Capital, Labour, and Enterprise), Part 2*, Cambridge, Cambridge University Press.

Chandler, A.D., and Hikino, T. (1997), The Large Industrial Enterprise and the Dynamics of Modern Economic Growth, in A.D. Chandler, F. Amatori and T. Hikino (eds), *Big Business and the Wealth of Nations*, Cambridge, Cambridge University Press.

Chang, H.-J., and Singh, A. (1997), Can Large Firms Be Run Efficiently Without Being Bureaucratic?, *Journal of International Development*, 9 (6), 865–75.

Coase, R.H. (1937), The Nature of the Firm, *Economica*, 4 (16), 386–405.

Coase, R.H. (1972), Industrial Organization: a Proposal for Research, in V.R. Fuchs (ed.), *Policy Issues and Research Opportunities in Industrial Organization*, New York, NBER.

Colombo, M.G. (ed.) (1998), *The Changing Boundaries of the Firm: Explaining Evolving Inter-Firm Relations*, London, Routledge.

Contini, B. (1984), Firm Size and the Division of Labor, *Banca Nazionale del Lavoro Quarterly Review*, 37 (151), 367–80.

Contini, B., and Revelli R. (1992), *Imprese, Occupazione e Retribuzioni al Microscopio*, Bologna, Il Mulino.

Cyert, R.M., and March, J.G. (1963), *A Behavioral Theory of the Firm*, New Jersey, Prentice-Hall (2nd edn 1992, Oxford, Basil Blackwell).

Das, B.J., Chappell, W.F., and Shughart II, W.F. (1993), Demand Fluctuations and Firm Heterogeneity, *Journal of Industrial Economics*, 41 (1), 51–60.

Davis, S.J., and Henrekson, M. (1999), Explaining National Differences in the Size and Industry Distribution of Employment, *Small Business Economics*, 12 (1), 59–83.

Deakin, S., and Wilkinson, F. (1996), Contracts, Cooperation and Trust: the Role of the Institutional Framework, in D. Campbell and P. Vincent-Jones (eds), *Contract and Economic Organisation: Socio-Legal Initiatives*, Aldershot, Dartmouth.

Department of Trade and Industry, Business Statistics Office (1971), *Report on the Census of Production 1968*, London, HMSO.

Didier, M. (1982), Crise et concentration du secteur productif, *Economie et Statistique*, no. 144, 3–12.

Didier, M., and Malinvaud, E. (1969), La concentration de l'industrie s'est-elle accentuée depuis le début du siècle?, *Economie et Statistique*, no. 2, 3–10.

Doi, N., and Cowling, M. (1998), The Evolution of Firm Size and Employment Share Distribution in Japanese and UK Manufacturing: a Study of Small Business Presence, *Small Business Economics*, 10 (3), 283–92.

Dosi, G. (1988), Sources, Procedures, and Microeconomic Effects of Innovation, *Journal of Economic Literature*, 26 (3), 1120–71.

Droucopoulos, V., and Thomadakis, S. (1993), The Share of Small and Medium-Sized Enterprise in Greek Manufacturing, *Small Business Economics*, 5 (3), 187–96.

Dunne, P., and Hughes, A. (1992), Large Firms, Small Firms, and the Changing Structure of the Competitive Industry in the 1980s, in C. Driver and P. Dunne (eds), *Structural Change in the UK Economy*, Cambridge, Cambridge University Press.

Eatwell, J. (1995), The International Origins of Unemployment, in J. Michie and J. Grieve-Smith (eds), *Managing the Global Economy*, Oxford, Oxford University Press.

Edwards, C.D. (1963), Size of Markets, Scale of Firms, and the Character of Competition, in E.A.G. Robinson (ed.), *Economic Consequences of the Size of Nations*, London, Macmillan.

Ehrlich, E. (1985), The Size Structure of Manufacturing Establishments and Enterprises: an International Comparison, *Journal of Comparative Economics*, 9 (3), 267–95.

Eurostat (various years), *Enterprises in Europe*, Luxembourg, Office for the Publications of the European Communities.

Ferrando, A., and Ganoulis, Y. (1999), Business Shocks e Dimensioni di Impresa [English translation available on request], in F. Traù (ed.), *La "questione dimensionale" nell'industria italiana*, Bologna, Il Mulino.

Foss, N.J., and Knudsen, C. (eds) (1996), *Towards a Competence Theory of the Firm*, London and New York, Routledge.

Fritsch, M. (1993), The Role of Small Firms in West Germany, in Z.J. Acs and D.B. Audretsch (eds), *Small Firms and Entrepreneurship: an East–West Perspective*, Cambridge, Cambridge University Press.

Galbraith, J.K. (1967), *The New Industrial State*, London, Hamish Hamilton.

Geroski, P.A. and Gugler, K.P. (2001), *Corporate Growth Convergence in Europe*, CEPR Discussion Papers, no. 238, June.

Glyn, A., Hughes, A., Lipietz, A., and Singh, A. (1990), The Rise and Fall of the Golden Age, in S.A. Marglin and G.B. Schor (eds), *The Golden Age of Capitalism: Interpreting the Postwar Experience*, Oxford, Clarendon Press.

Guelfi, A., and Traù, F. (1999), 'Confronti internazionali di dati censuari: aspetti metodologici e riscontri empirici', paper presented at the Meeting of the Italian Statistical Society, University of Udine, 7–9 June, now in E. Gori E., Giovannini and N. Batic (eds), *Verso i censimenti del 2000*, Udine, Ed. Forum, 2000.

Haire, M. (1959), Biological Models and Empirical Histories in the Growth of Organizations, in M. Haire (ed.), *Modern Organization Theory*, New York, Wiley and Sons.

Harrigan, K.R. (1983), *Strategies for Vertical Integration*, Lexington, MA, Gower Publishing.

Hart, O.E., and Moore, J. (1990), Property Rights and the Nature of the Firm, *Journal of Political Economy*, 98 (6), 1119–1158.

Henley, A. (1994), Industrial Deconcentration in UK Manufacturing Since 1980, *The Manchester School*, 62 (1), 40–59.

Hughes, A. (1987), Managerial Capitalism, entry in J. Eatwell, M. Milgate and P. Newman (eds), *The New Palgrave*, London, Macmillan.

Hughes, A. (1993), Industrial Concentration and Small Firms in the United Kingdom: the 1980s in Historical Perspective, in Z.J. Acs and D.B. Audretsch (eds), *Small Firms and Entrepreneurship: an East–West Perspective*, Cambridge, Cambridge University Press.

Hughes, A., and Singh, A. (1980), Mergers, Concentration, and Competition in Advanced Capitalist Economies: an International Perspective, in D.C. Mueller (ed.), *The Determinants and Effects of Mergers*, Cambridge, MA, Oelgeschlager, Gunn & Hain.

INSEE (1967), *Recensement de l'Industrie 1963, Resultats pour 1962*, Série Structures, vol. III, Paris, Imprimerie Nationale.

INSEE (1996), *Images Économiques des Entreprise au 1.1.1995*, vol. 1, Paris, Imprimerie Nationale.

ISTAT (1962), *Censimento Generale dell'Industria e del Commercio 1961*, vols. I and III, Roma.

Jensen, M., and Meckling, W. (1976), Theory of the Firm: Managerial Behavior, Agency Costs, and Ownership Structure, *Journal of Financial Economics*, 3 (4), 305–60.

Jewkes, J. (1952), The Size of the Factory, *Economic Journal*, 62 (146), 237–52.

Kaldor, N. (1934), The Equilibrium of the Firm, *Economic Journal*, 44 (173), 60–76.

Kaldor, N. (1966), *Causes of the Slow Rate of Economic Growth in the United Kingdom*, Cambridge, Cambridge University Press.

Kay, J. (2001), What Became of the New Economy?, *National Institute Economic Review*, 177, 56–69.

Kocka, J. (1978), Germany, in P. Mathias and M.M. Postan (eds), *Cambridge Economic History of Europe, Vol. VII (The Industrial Economies. Capital, Labour, and Enterprise), Part 1*, Cambridge, Cambridge University Press.

Kindleberger, C. (1958), *Economic Development*, New York, McGraw-Hill.

Landes, D.S. (1984), What Do Bosses Do?, *Journal of Economic History*, 46 (3), 585–623.

Leibenstein, H. (1976), *Beyond Economic Man: a New Foundation for Microeconomics*, Cambridge MA and London, Harvard University Press.

Loasby, B. (1994), Organisational Capabilities and Interfirm Relations, *Metroeconomica*, 45 (3), 248–65.

Maddigan, R.J. (1981), The Measurement of Vertical Integration, *Review of Economics and Statistics*, 63 (3), 328–35.

Malmgren, H.B. (1961), Information, Expectations and the Theory of the Firm, *Quarterly Journal of Economics*, 75 (3), 399–421.

Mansfield, E. (1992), Flexible Manufacturing Systems: Economic Effects in Japan, United States, and Western Europe, *Japan and the World Economy*, 4 (1), 1–16.

Marris, R. (1964), *The Economic Theory of Managerial Capitalism*, London, Macmillan.

Marris, R., and Wood, A. (eds) (1971), *The Corporate Economy*, London and Basingstoke, Macmillan.

Marshall, A. (1920), *Principles of Economics*, 8th edn, London, Macmillan.

Marx, K. (1977), *Capital. A Critique of Political Economy*, vol. I, New York, Random House Vintage Books.

Matthews, R.C.O. (1982), *Slower Growth in the Western World*, London, Heinemann.

Mayo, E. (1933), *The Human Problems of an Industrial Civilization*, Boston, Harvard Business School.

Meade, J.E. (1968), Is the New Industrial State Inevitable?, *Economic Journal*, 78 (310), 372–92.

Meager, N. (1992), Does Unemployment Lead to Self-Employment?, *Small Business Economics*, 4 (2), 87–103.

Mills, D.E., and Schumann, L. (1985), Industry Structure with Fluctuating Demand, *American Economic Review*, 75 (4), 758–67.

Momigliano, F. (1971), Prefazione, in G. Ruffolo, *La grande impresa nella società moderna*, Torino, Einaudi.

Montgomery, C. (1994), Corporate Diversification, *Journal of Economic Perspectives*, 8 (3), 163–78.

OECD (1985), Employment in Small and Large Firms: Where Have the Jobs Come From?, *Employment Outlook* (ch. 4), September, Paris, OECD.

Oi, W.J. (1962), Labor as a Quasi-Fixed Factor, *Journal of Political Economy*, 70 (6), 538–55.

Olson, M. (1987), Diseconomies of Scale and Development, *The Cato Journal*, 7 (1), 77–97.

Ouchi, W.G. (1980), Markets, Bureaucracies, and Clans, *Administrative Science Quarterly*, 25 (1), 129–41.

Papandreou, A.G. (1952), Some Basic Problems in the Theory of the Firm, in B.F. Haley, *A Survey of Contemporary Economics*, Homewood, IL, R.D. Irwin.

Penrose, E.T. (1980), *The Theory of the Growth of the Firm*, Oxford, Basil Blackwell.

Piore, M.J., and Sabel, C.F. (1984), *The Second Industrial Divide*, New York, Basic Books.

Postan, M.M. (1967), *An Economic History of Western Europe, 1945–1964*, London, Methuen and Co.

Powell, W.W. (1990), Neither Market nor Hierarchy: Networks Forms of Organization, *Research in Organizational Behavior*, 12, 295–336.

Prais, S.J. (1981) [1976], *The Evolution of Giant Firms in Britain*, Cambridge, Cambridge University Press.

Pryor, F.L. (1972), The Size of Production Establishments in Manufacturing, *Economic Journal*, 82 (326), 547–66.

Pryor, F.L. (2001), Will Most of Us Be Working for Giant Enterprises by 2028?, *Journal of Economic Behaviour and Organization*, 44, 363–82.

Putterman, L. (1986), The Economic Nature of the Firm: an Overview, in L. Putterman (ed.), *The Economic Nature of the Firm: a Reader*, Cambridge, Cambridge University Press.

Radner, R. (1992), Hierarchy: the Economics of Managing, *Journal of Economic Literature*, 30 (3), 1382–1415.

Reder, M.W. (1947), A Reconsideration of the Marginal Productivity Theory, *Journal of Political Economy*, 55 (5), 450–8.

Richardson, G.B. (1960), *Information and Investment*, Oxford, Oxford University Press (2nd edn. Clarendon Press, 1990).

Richardson, G.B. (1964), The Limits to a Firm's Rate of Growth, *Oxford Economic Papers*, 16 (1), 9–23.

Richardson, G.B. (1972), The Organisation of Industry, *Economic Journal*, 82 (327), 883–96.

Robertson, D.H. (1928), *The Control of Industry*, Cambridge, Nisbet and Co., Cambridge University Press.

Robinson, E.A.G. (1934), The Problem of Management and the Size of the Firm, *Economic Journal*, 44 (174), 242–57.

Robinson, E.A.G. (1935), *The Structure of Competitive Industry*, Cambridge, Nisbet and Co., Cambridge University Press.

Robson, G.B., and Gallagher, C.C. (1994), Change in the Size Distribution of UK Firms, *Small Business Economics*, 6 (4), 299–312.

Sargant Florence, P. (1954), The Size of the Factory: a Reply, *Economic Journal*, 64 (255), 625–8.

Sato, Y. (1989), Small Business in Japan: a Historical Perspective, *Small Business Economics*, 1 (2), 121–8.

Schrader, D.E. (1993), *The Corporation as Anomaly*, Cambridge, Cambridge University Press.

Schwalbach, J. (1990), Small Business in German Manufacturing, in Z.J. Acs and D.B. Audretsch (eds), *The Economics of Small Firms: a European Challenge*, Dordrecht, Kluwer.

Schwalbach, J. (1994), Small Business Dynamics in Europe, *Small Business Economics*, 6 (1), 21–5.

Sengenberger, W., Loveman, G.W., and Piore, M.J. (eds) (1990), *The Re-emergence of Small Enterprises: Industrial Restructuring in Industrialised Countries*, Geneva, International Institute for Labour Studies.

Simon, H.A. (1945), *Administrative Behavior*, New York, The Free Press (Last edn, 1997).

Simon, H.A. (1991), Organizations and Markets, *Journal of Economic Perspectives*, 5 (2), 25–44.

Singh, A. (1997), Liberalization and Globalization: an Unhealthy Euphoria, in J. Michie and J. Grieve-Smith (eds), *Employment and Economic Performance*, Oxford, Oxford University Press.

Sloan, A.P., Jr (1963), *My Years with General Motors*, New York, Doubleday and Co.

Smith, A. (1963), *An Inquiry into the Nature and Causes of the Wealth of Nations*, ed. M. Blaug, Homewood, IL, R.D. Irwin.

Smyth, D.J., Boyes, W.J., and Peseau D.E. (1975), *Size, Growth, Profits and Executive Compensation in the Large Corporation: a Study of the 500 Largest United Kingdom and United States Industrial Corporations*, London and Basingstoke, Macmillan.

Spilling, O.R. (1988), On the Re-Emergence of Small Scale Production: the Norwegian Case in International Comparison, *Small Business Economics*, 10 (4), 401–17.

Sraffa, P. (1926), The Laws of Returns under Competitive Conditions, *Economic Journal*, 36 (144), 535–50.

Stanworth, J., and Gray, C. (1991), *Bolton 20 Years On: the Small Firm in the 1990s*, London, Paul Chapman.

Statistics Bureau (1996), *1994 Establishment Directory Maintenance Survey of Japan*, Part 1, Tokyo, Management and Coordination Agency.

Statistisches Bundesamt (1966), *Zensus im Produzierenden Gewerbe 1962*, Heft 1, Stuttgart, W. Kohlhammer GMBH.

Statistisches Bundesamt (various years), *Betriebe, Beschäftigte und Umsatz im Bergbau und im Verarbeitenden Gewerbe nach Beschäftigtengrößenklassen 1977 and 1990*, Stuttgart, W. Kohlhammer GMBH and Metzler Poeschel.

Statistisches Bundesamt (various years), *Kostenstruktur der Unternehmen im Bergbau und Verarbeitenden Gewerbe, 1977, 1990*, Reihe: 4.3.1; 4.3.2; 4.3.3, Stuttgart, W. Kohlhammer GMBH and Metzler Poeschel.

Steindl, J. (1945), *Small and Big Business*, Oxford, Basil Blackwell (2nd edn 1990, London and Basingstoke, Macmillan).

Stigler, G.J. (1939), Production and Distribution in the Short Run, *Journal of Political Economy*, 47 (3), 305–27.

Stockmann, R., and Leicht, R. (1994), The Pattern of Changes in the Long-Term Development of Establishment Size, *Small Business Economics*, 6 (6), 451–63.

Storey, D.J. (1994), *Understanding the Small Business Sector*, London, Routledge.

Traù, F. (1996), Why Do Firms Grow?, *ESRC Centre for Business Research Working Paper Series*, no. 26, University of Cambridge, March.

Traù, F. (1997), Recent Trends in the Size Structure of Italian Manufacturing Firms, *Small Business Economics*, 9 (3), 273–85.

Traù, F. (1998), Structural Change and Firms' Propensity to Grow in Italian Manufacturing, *Discussion Papers in Economics and Management*, Series A, vol. 10, Department of Economics, University of Reading, February.

Traù, F. (ed) (1999), *La 'Questione Dimensionale' nell'Industria Italiana*, Bologna, Il Mulino.

Traù, F. (2000), The Rise and Fall of the Size of Firms, *ESRC Centre for Business Research Working Paper Series*, no. 156, University of Cambridge, March.

Traù, F. (2001), The Macroeconomic Environment and the Size Pattern of Business Firms, *ESRC Centre for Business Research Working Paper Series*, no. 192, University of Cambridge, March (Italian version in *L'industria. Rivista di Economia e Politica Industriale*, 22 (1), 173–204).

Tuck, R.H. (1954), *An Essay in the Economic Theory of Rank*, Oxford, Basil Blackwell.

United Nations (1953), *Studies in Methods: Industrial Censuses and Related Enquiries*, Series F, no. 4, vols. I and II, Statistical Office of the United Nations, Department of Economic Affairs, New York.

United Nations (1960), *International Recommendations on the 1963 World Programme of Basic Industrial Statistics*, Statistical Papers, Series M, no. 17 (Rev. 1 Add. 1), Statistical Office of the United Nations, Department of Economic and Social Affairs, New York.

US Department of Commerce, Bureau of the Census (various years), *Enterprise Statistics 1963, 1972, 1982, 1992*, Washington DC, US Government Printing Office.

US Department of Commerce, Bureau of the Census (various years), *Census of Manufactures 1963, 1992*, Washington DC, US Government Printing Office.

Utton, M.A. (1971), The Effects of Mergers on Concentration: UK Manufacturing Industry, 1954–65, *Journal of Industrial Economics*, 20 (1), 42–58.

van Ark, B., and Monnikhof, E. (1996), Size Distribution of Output and Employment: a Data Set for Manufacturing Industries in Five OECD Countries, 1960s–1990, *Economics Department Working Papers*, no. 166, Paris, OECD.

Vercelli, A. (1988), Technological Flexibility, Financial Fragility and the Recent Revival of Schumpeterian Entrepreneurship, *Recherches Economiques de Louvain*, 54 (1), 103–32.

Williamson, O.E. (1964), *The Economics of Discretionary Behavior: Managerial Objectives in a Theory of the Firm*, Englewood Cliffs, NJ, Prentice-Hall.

Williamson, O.E. (1967), Hierarchical Control and Optimum Firm Size, *Journal of Political Economy*, 75 (2), 123–38.

Williamson, O.E. (1970), *Corporate Control and Business Behaviour*, Englewood Cliffs, NJ, Prentice-Hall.

Williamson, O.E. (1971), Managerial Discretion, Organization Form, and the Multi-division Hypothesis, in R. Marris and A. Wood (eds), *The Corporate Economy*, London and Basingstoke, Macmillan.

Williamson, O.E. (1993), The Logic of Economic Organization, in O.E. Williamson and S.G. Winter (eds), *The Nature of the Firm: Origins, Evolution and Development*, New York, Oxford University Press.

Woodward, J. (1965), *Industrial Organization: Theory and Practice*, London, Oxford University Press.

Index